THE GOSPEL OF
OUR MOTHER GOD

Rejoice, poor wanderers of the earth and exiles from the house of your Mother, for to you shall come a Guide and a Deliverer.

MYTHOS OF GOD THE DAUGHTER
CH. 2, V. 12

The Gospel of
Our Mother God

*The Scriptures of
the World's First Faith*

THE GOLDEN ORDER PRESS

THE GOLDEN ORDER PRESS
publications@mother-god.com

Approved for distribution in
The Celestial Empire of Aristasia
And all Imperial Dependencies.

1st Edition
demy 8vo

Table of Contents

Should serpents lie athwart your path
Exhaling noxious smoke and flame,
One thought of Kwan Yin's saving power
Would make them vanish fast as sound.

Should thunder roll and lightning flash,
Or fearsome rains come hissing down,
One thought of Kwan Yin's saving power
Would straightway lull the storm.

Though beings oppressed by karmic woes
Endure innumerable sorrows,
Kwan Yin's miraculous perception
Enables Her to purge them all.

Imbued with supernatural power
And wise in using skillful means,
In every corner of the world,
She manifests her countless forms.

No matter what black evils gather
What hell-spawned demons, savage beasts,
What ills of birth, age, sickness, death,
Kwan Yin will one by one destroy them.

True Kwan Yin! Pure Kwan Yin!
Immeasurably wise Kwan Yin!
Merciful and filled with pity,
Ever longed for and revered!

O Radiance spotless and effulgent!
O night-dispelling Sun of Wisdom!
O Vanquisher of storm and flame!
Your glory fills the world!

LOTUS SUTRA

Introduction

THE FAITH of Our Mother God consists in the acceptance of our Mother-Creatrix as the one Supreme Being, the Source and Origin of all that is, the One without a second, upon Whom the existence of anything whatever is absolutely dependent. To know this and to love Her—or even to wish to love Her—is the whole of our religion in its essence.

Our Faith is the oldest in the world and long predates the time when words were written down. The words of the first Age were closer to the words of Angels, and only much later were the Truths of religion expressed in words or ideas anything like our own. Over the millennia, those words and ideas have crystallised into what we may call a Gospel. And while there has never been a "Bible" for devotees of Our Mother God, we feel the time has now come when such a book is needed.

We begin the book with the Filianic Creed, which, while it is not strictly Scripture, provides a thealogical framework within which we may understand all the Scriptures that are to follow.

The Filianic Creed naturally expresses Filianic doctrine in its purest form and may be said to be a complete summary of the Filianic faith. Not all devotees of Our Mother God are Filianists, but most pure Déanists (worshipers of the Mother alone) recognise that the Daughter-Aspect—the Saviour—is a fundamental Face of Our Mother, as is Her supra-formal, supra-personal Aspect which Filianists call the Dark Mother. One does not need to have an explicit Trinitarian doctrine in order to understand this or to see the value of the Filianic Creed to all believers.

The Threefold Nature of Dea, however, is long established in history and tradition. The so-called "triple Goddess" is found throughout the world, and while superficial observers may imagine the doctrine that God is Three in One and One in three to be "borrowed from Christianity", history shows clearly that it is actually Christianity that borrowed this doctrine from the world's oldest religion.

In presenting some of the Sanskrit writings that incorporate the ancient traditions of Our Mother God, the commentaries show how the three Aspects of Dea are always present, "eternally distinct yet intimately entwined", whether an explicit Trinitarianism is in question or not.

The first section of the book consists of fundamental Mythic accounts. The term "myth" is much misunderstood in the modern West and often taken to be a synonym for "untruth", but myths are, in fact, the supra-historical stories that depict the underlying Truths of our very existence. These exact versions of our Mythos are of relatively recent origin, but their roots go back to the dawn of history. They are the tales that have been told and told again from the time of our First Mothers and they lie at the bedrock not only of the human *psyche* but of the manifest cosmos itself.

The final major section of this book consists of the Filianic Sutras, again of relatively recent origin in this precise form but again transmitting the timeless wisdom of the world's first Faith. As with the Mythos, these are "Authorised Versions", meaning that they have been carefully examined in the light of traditional doctrine. Different existing versions have been compared and where accretions from modern New Age and other non-traditional schools of thought have crept in, these have been eliminated. Doubtful texts have not been included. Our aim has been to transmit a pure and reliable Gospel that may be trusted as the clear wellspring of the most ancient and perfect Truth.

We wish this book to be in the hands of pure devotees everywhere and our watchword has been purity rather than quantity. Those who live by this Gospel may be few, but as it is written in the Sutra of *The Heart of Water*:

For though in this place thou seemest but a few, and Her servants reduced to a remnant, yet in truth the age of the unbelievers is but a moment in the endless stream of time... In truth thou art surrounded by the bright host of Her children, serried through time and space, in whose light the unbelievers are but the remnant of a remnant, and their world but a cobweb in the midst of a glittering palace.

THE HEART OF WATER 25-27

The Filianic Creed

I believe that I am created
from before the dawn of time
by the one eternal Dea.

I believe that Dea is One
and there are none beside Her,
And I believe that She is also Three.

I believe in the Mother,
Who is pure Light,
the Creatrix of the earth and of the heavens
and of all the illimitable cosmos.

And I believe in Her virgin Daughter,
born of the virgin Mother,
the Ruler of all the energies of creation,
Whose nature is perfect Love.

And I believe in She that stands beyond these Two,
Whose Name has not been spoken on this earth:
For She is the Beginning and the End;
the First Principle and the Final Cause;
the unoriginated Origin of being.

I believe that I was made a perfect creature
and at the dawn of time my soul did turn
from the Perfection of existence
in the infirmity of her sovereign will:
And through this fault do I suffer
the limitation of imperfect being.

I believe that the Daughter of Eternity
gave herself to be cast down into darkness and death.

I believe that She rose from death triumphant
And reigns as Queen of Heaven.

I believe that through Her death
the fault of my soul shall perish,
And I believe, through Her triumphant life,
My soul shall rise renewed in her perfection
that she may return to eternal communion
with the one eternal Dea.

The Filianic Creed is not in itself a Scripture, but we begin this
book with it because it provides a thealogical framework for all
that follows. While the Trinitarian thealogy of the Creed may
not be regarded "literally" by all non-Filianic believers (but then
the question of "literalness" does not arise for us as it does for
Christians) it may be accepted by all as the fundamental statement of the Nature of Deity in Her primary Aspects and of the
quest of the human soul.

Commentary
A brief explanation of the Eight Statements of the Filianic Creed.

**I believe that I am created
from before the dawn of time
by the one eternal Dea.**

Thus begins what, on the microcosmic level, can be called the
history of the soul and, on the macrocosmic level, the history of
time.

It makes clear the eternal nature of the soul and of her Creatrix.

Each of us has always existed as a fragment of the All-
Reality that is God the Mother. She is our true Home and
Point of Origin.

When time began and *things* existed in separation from
God, the separation of individual existence also became possible, with all its attendant joys and suffering.

This first statement of the Creed also makes clear the fact that Dea comes first: before all things; before time; before being itself.

Many modern people try to explain God as a creation of the human mind. But She created the human mind as well as every other thing in existence. If there are certain similarities between our ideas of the Divine and ourselves, it is because we originated in Dea; not because Dea originated in us. This First Statement gives the conclusive answer of the devotee to all "psychological explanations of religion". God does not come from our minds; our minds come from God.

**I believe that Dea is One
and there are none beside Her,
And I believe that She is also Three.**

That God is One and also Three is the central statement of Trinitarian doctrine. The Christian theologian St. Augustine mocked pagan worshippers of the "Triple Goddess" for believing that God the Mother is One and also Three, but after his conversion came to defend the patriarchal version of the same doctrine.

The statement that there are none beside Her makes it clear that Dea is the one Supreme Being: the Absolute. There can no more be two Absolutes than a circle can have two centres.

While we believe that Dea has many Names and Aspects, and also believe that there are great Angelic Beings (or Janyati) who do Her work, the thing which certain patriarchal religions like to term "polytheism", or the belief that there can be more than one God, is a metaphysical absurdity that no authentic religious tradition has ever believed.

"Polytheism" in the sense that Christians and Moslems use it, is no more than a semantic confusion. Some languages use terms like *thea*, *devi* or *dea* to mean both the Supreme Being and Her lesser aspects. This has never—except possibly at very degenerate stages of certain cultures—implied that there could

11

be more than one Supreme Being, which would clearly be both spiritually and metaphysically absurd.

"There are none beside Her" also rules out the male "consorts" introduced by some patriarchal and semi-patriarchal cults. Since Dea is the Absolute, She can have no consort, for She Herself is All in All.

I believe in the Mother,
Who is pure Light.
the Creatrix of the earth and of the heavens
and of all the illimitable cosmos.

The First Person of the Holy Trinity is God the Mother. She is the first thing that we can know, for before Her there is no time and no space: no things of any sort. She is the Creatrix of all, the origin of everything we can know.

She is Light, because without Her nothing would be visible. She is the Supreme Intelligence (*mati*) or Light of the universe. She is the Supreme Consciousness. Every other consciousness is but a fragment of Her Consciousness.

Just as the sun is the source of all light in our world (the moon's light is the reflected light of the sun, and even fire is only the release of the solar energy that made possible the growth of wood or other combustible material), so the Supernal Sun is the source of all spiritual Light. God the Mother is that Supernal Sun.

All things, both earthly and heavenly, begin in God the Mother. She is both the Origin of all things and the Light by which we see them. All true science must begin with Dea, which is why thealogy is called the Queen of the Sciences.

And I believe in Her virgin Daughter,
born of the virgin Mother,
the Ruler of all the energies of creation,
Whose nature is perfect Love.

As maid was separated from Dea, Her absolute Light became "too great for us to look upon". Thus, in Her infinite compassion, She gave birth to a Daughter Who was "not separate from Her, but One with Her, and the Child of Her Light".

Just as we cannot look upon the sun but the moon reflects the solar light in a radiance we may gaze upon, so the Daughter reflects the Light of the Mother upon us in a gentle form. A form tempered kindly to our human frailty.

The Daughter mediates the Light of the Mother not only to maid, but to all creation. Strictly, a creation that existed in separation from Dea could not exist, for She is its sole Source of being; yet creation (or manifestation) itself is by definition the development of *things* other than God.

The Daughter resolves this paradox by mediating the Divine Light to a non-Divine creation. Thus she is the Preserver of the Worlds and the controller (*thamë*) of all the lesser energies that sustain them in being.

Since this is the supreme Act of Compassion, the Daughter is called pure Love (*sushuri*) just as the Mother is pure Light (*mati*).

The two radiances of the sun are warmth and light. In traditional pictures that show the sun's rays as alternately straight and wavy, the straight lines represent light and the wavy lines represent warmth.

Thus, while the Mother and the Daughter are the Supernal Sun and the Supernal Moon respectively, their Divine Activity may also, on a certain level, be regarded as the two solar Functions. The Mother is the Supreme Light, or Intelligence, and the Daughter the Supreme Love, or Warmth.

The stress upon the virginity of both Mother and Daughter emphasises the fact that they are beyond material manifestation (though they are its sole Cause) and also refutes the patriarchal and semi-patriarchal cults that have invented a male consort for either Mother or Daughter.

**And I believe in She that stands beyond these Two,
Whose Name has not been spoken on this earth:**

For She is the Beginning and the End:
the First Principle and the Final Cause;
the unoriginated Origin of being.

The Dark Mother is so called because we can know nothing of Her. It does *not* indicate a morally negative or "dark" nature. As with the Upanishadic doctrine of the Absolute, we can only say of Her *neti, neti*: "not that, nor that". Or as the Chinese formulation has it: "The Tao that can be spoken is not the true Tao". She is the true Object of all that is called "negative thealogy".

While the Light of God the Mother reveals all that is humanly comprehensible, the Darkness of the Dark Mother conceals all that is beyond mortal understanding. In truth, though, it conceals nothing, for the seeming-darkness is really only our inability to see, so long as we remain upon the Wheel of werdë—the flux of *samsara*.

In the Filianic Rite She is called "Dark beyond the Light and Light beyond the Darkness" because She is that which lies beyond the bright Light even of our dear Mother, and yet within Her apparent Darkness lies the greatest Light of all.

From the human perspective, She is the Third Person of the Trinity, but from the Celestial perspective, She is the First Person.

These paradoxes do not need to trouble us, for the beautiful Light of the Mother and the all-nurturing Love of the Daughter are the proper objects of our devotion.

Indeed, we would treat with great caution any who claimed to be a follower of the Dark Mother unless she showed signs of truly exceptional spiritual advancement and complete detachment from the things of this world.

I believe that I was made a perfect creature
and at the dawn of time my soul did turn
from the Perfection of existence
in the infirmity of her sovereign will:
And through this fault do I suffer
the limitation of imperfect being.

Having declared our faith in the Holy Trinity, we return to the History of the Soul, begun in the First Statement of the Creed.

Every spiritual tradition agrees that the Problem of Maid is her separation from the Absolute. Buddhism speaks of the suffering (*dukkha*) caused by our being bound to the worlds of relativity and change (*samsara*). The Abrahamic traditions speak of the loss of the Garden of Eden. Hindus strive for union (*yoga*) with the Absolute, which, they would fervently agree, is actually a re-union.

Here the Filianic Creed speaks of the Problem of Maid. It speaks of our original perfection and of our turning from Dea. That turning is a complex thealogical question which we will not attempt to discuss fully here.

Different traditions regard this separation—the Problem of Maid—differently. Eastern traditions (and the ancient Greeks) see it as an intellectual problem—one of knowledge and ignorance. More recent Western traditions (and Islam) have tended to see it as a moral problem—one of right or wrong *will*.

Actually, this is more a matter of emphasis, as both perspectives are found in all traditions. The knowledge-perspective tends to correspond to the Path of Light (*jnana marga*, path of Sai Mati), that is, to the Intellectual approach to Dea; while the will-(or moral) perspective tends to correspond to the Path of Love (*bhakti marga*, path of Sai Sushuri).

Filianic religion, being centred on the Daughter, Who is Pure Love, leans toward the will-interpretation of the Problem of Maid. The phrase "in the infirmity of her sovereign will" clearly indicates this.

However, both perspectives are strongly present in Déanic religion. To some extent the knowledge-perspective is more common in those whose primary devotion is to the Mother (even though this may be a Love-path too) and the will-perspective more common in those whose primary devotion is to the Daughter

Nonetheless, there is no radical separation between Mother-devotion and Daughter-devotion or between the Light-path and the Love-path, and all of us can make this Statement of the Creed in full conscience.

**I believe that the Daughter of Eternity
gave Herself to be cast down into darkness and death.
I believe that She rose from death triumphant
And reigns as Queen of Heaven.**

With beautiful simplicity and brevity, this Statement tells the story of the Daughter's Sacrifice. The cycle of the Divine Acts of the Daughter is thus encapsulated in the Creed, beginning with the Nativity in the Fourth Statement and continuing here to the Sacrifice of Eastre and the Exaltation of the Queen of Heaven. In the Cycle of the Year these events take place in the "Daughter half" of the year consisting of Winter and Spring:
• The Nativity is celebrated at midwinter.
• The Daughter's Taking on of Fate (equivalent to the Vow of Quan Yin* and stated here in the words "gave Herself") at the Feast of Lights—the "Candlemas" cross-quarter day in early February.
• Her Death and Resurrection come at Eastre, the Spring Equinox.
• Her Exaltation as the Queen of Heaven at the cross-quarter known as May-Day.
The whole Sacred Drama, the fundamental feminine story of the Divine Sacrifice, is told in this Statement, so that, in a few simple words, we may assert our faith in the Primordial Mystery.

**I believe that through Her death
the fault of my soul shall perish,
And I believe, through Her triumphant life,
My soul shall rise renewed in her perfection
that she may return to eternal communion
with the One eternal Dea.**

* i.e to abstain from Liberation until every being is saved, "even to the last blade of Grass". Quan Yin thus, while being Divine, reduces Herself to human level, and in many of Her Legends suffers death and liberates Hell, even as the Daughter does in the Filianic Mythos: for we are dealing not with random "fables" but with Primordial Truth.

16

This final Statement of the Creed weaves together, again with astonishing brevity, all the threads that have been spun. The History of the Soul is concluded. The Problem of Maid has its true resolution. The Sacred Drama of the Divine Sacrifice ends with its triumphant victory over maid's suffering. The Trinity, having been adored in each of Her Persons, is again seen in the perspective of Her fundamental Unity; and all things are resolved in that Final Blissful Union in which all beings are saved, "even to the last blade of grass".

The Filianic Creed expresses, in the most concise and elegant manner, the whole essence of the Filianic faith. If one learns the Creed, one knows the religion, even though many more pages of commentary might be written than the few simple expositions we have attempted to give here.

But the Creed is more than an intellectual tool. It is in itself an act of devotion, expressing our faith, our love and our adoration. and reminding us each of the journey of her own soul and of the infinite kindness and compassion of Dea.

The Creed of Dea can be summed up in one simple statement:

I believe in God the Mother.

If you can make this statement and you also love Her—or even want to love Her—then you have all that is necessary.

The Filianic Creed expands this simple "I believe" into a much greater—but still simple—statement of the entire Sacred Drama, from Creation to final Redemption, and of the pure doctrine of the Holy Feminine Trinity.

Part I

FUNDAMENTAL MYTHOS

WE LIVE in a world of time and space. With our ordinary consciousness, we are unable to understand anything outside space-time.

Certain contemplative states permit maid to transcend her normal limitations (this is what is properly termed Pure Intellect as opposed to material reason) but for most people, most of the time, the world of time and space is the only one we can understand. Even the contemplative, if she wishes to communicate her vision, must couch it in the language of space-time "events", because these are the only things our language is equipped to deal with.

Thus extra-temporal events are depicted in myth as if they were temporal events. To take a very obvious example, the creation of the world is depicted as if it were taking place *in* space-time, when clearly it is the *origin* of space-time and cannot be within it.

Miss Alice Lucy Trent has said "History depicts events that may or may not have happened, while myth depicts, in terms of 'events', things that *cannot not be*."

Once the modern Western mind has understood this, another problem arises. She is prone to say "Oh, so this isn't *really* what happened. It is just a story."

But myth *is* really what happened, told in the only form in which we can understand it.

Many traditional peoples have more than one creation story. Some Déanists, for example, have stories in which the creation was hatched by the Mother from the World-Egg. Anyone who has worked with, say, Asian peoples who are not too thoroughly Westernised, will be aware that questions of "which myth is true" never even arise. The naïvety with which the materialistic Western mind can *only* understand myth as if it were either history or poetry is unknown to them.

Western "fundamentalism", which wishes to reduce myth to history, is as misconceived as the skepticism it arose to combat—which wishes to "refute" myth by proving that it is *not* history.

We Déanists, as a traditional people and a people that has suffered the re-writing of its fundamental Mythos by the patriarchy, find the following re-tellings of the most fundamental Mythos to be the most effective way of approaching Truth at this time in history.

We do not claim that these texts are word-for-word Divinely inspired and the only possible telling of the Truths (nor do we credit similar claims for certain patriarchal texts). We *do* accept them as fully adequate and providentially guided iterations of the fundamental Mythos in a form emotionally and spiritually suited to the soul of Western maid in the late Kali Yuga.

The story of the Saviour—Her birth, Her taking-on of fate, Her death, Her harrowing of hell, Her resurrection and Her exaltation as Queen of Heaven—long predates Christianity and is feminine in its original forms.

We do not see this in terms of an historical *avatara* at a particular time and place in earthly history. Such historical reflections of this fundamental Truth that underlies the very existence of the universe may well have taken place, but our concern is with the *fundamental* Mythos that underlies any and all time-bound reflections.

The following mythic accounts, in this precise form, are, to the best of our knowledge, around thirty years old at the time of writing. The claim that they are, *in this precise form*, of pre-patriarchal origin must, we feel, be dismissed. The human mind undergoes changes over the great world-eras and all traditions have necessarily been adapted to the particular form of humanity that inhabits the latter millennia of Kali Yuga.

However, we do accept that such claims, or beliefs, are a way of expressing the real truth about this Mythos: that it is providentially adapted to convey to us, in our current condition, the spiritual understanding that our earliest foremothers possessed.

That it is, in other words, the Truth.

The Creation

Authorised Version

Chapter One

BEFORE and beyond all things is the Mistress of All Things, and when nothing was, She was. 2. And having no solid place that Her feet might rest upon, She divided the sea from the sky, and made a dance of solitary splendour upon the crested deeps. 3. And She was pure consciousness or energy, and therefore pure delight; and the crashing of the waves was the overflowing of Her joy. 4. And the white force of Her superabundant joy grew so great that it must take shape in laughter; and Her laughter was the shape of all things. 5. For each peal of Her voice became a golden fragment, broken from the Whole and yet complete in itself. And She loved each fragment with all the joy of Her being. And Her hands knew cunning. 6. And She stretched forth Her hands and gave a shape to each fragment, and no one was like any other. 7. And She parted the vasty waters that there might be a place to set them down.

And She laughed.

8. And each fragment was filled with Her delight, and therefore was living. And some grew in the deep earth, and were plants and trees; some ran about the ground or flew above it; and those first-made that had no place to be set down became the fishes and the creatures of the sea. And every thing was golden.

And She laughed.

9. And at the edges, where the waters had been parted, they lay still and shallow; and there She cast Her gaze. And She saw an image of Herself, all suffused in the light of love and energy. And She laughed. 10. And as She laughed, the image rose up from the water and stood before Her. And this was the first of Her daughters. And she was filled with love for Her, and therefore was the first creature of Spirit. 11. And she knew cunning,

and she ran about the earth with love of all things, giving a name to every thing and creature, each in the order that She had shaped them.

12. And the Mistress of All Things was filled with delight, and ran laughing through the forests of the earth. 13. And every peal of Her voice became the image of a golden fragment of Her Spirit. 14. And the trees and rivers were filled with nymphs and every kind of sprite. And all were Her daughters. And Her love for each was inexhaustible, for each was a reflection of some boundless fragment of Her unbounded Spirit. 15. And all their multitude did not exhaust the number of the fragments of Her Spirit. 16. And to each was given the governance of some earthly thing.

Chapter Two

BUT one there was that had not been shaped by Her, and that was not Her daughter, nor a creature of Spirit. But this was the space between the fragments and the nothingness that had been before things were. It had not energy nor delight, but only weight. It had not shape, but could only coil and uncoil itself about the things that were. It was the Snake, and was not golden, but black.

2. The Snake hated all the things that had become, and hated the separation of the waters and the sky. It hated light and energy, desiring all to be darkness and nothingness.

3. And when the world had lived a time in joy (though what that time was none can say, for then were neither days nor nights, nor moons to tell the month), the Snake came to the first of the daughters of the Mistress of All Things, and coiled about her feet and spoke to her, saying:

4. First of the daughters of creation, you have lived a time that cannot be counted, and have run for all that time in the footsteps of the Mother, and have never taken rest among the things that are. Only embrace me and you shall have that rest.

5. A long time she listened to the words of the Snake. She did not know what rest might be, but knew that it was not of

Her. 6. And yet so enticingly did the Snake speak of the sweetness of rest, surpassing all delight, that at last she threw herself down and embraced it. 7. And because she was suffused with the delight of the Mistress of All Things, the Snake immediately took on shape. 8. And its shape was like to hers, but its body was filled with weight, and was barren, for being not a creature of Spirit, it had not the power of creation.

9. And at once she was turned from the Light of the Mother to the lights of the things that are. And she became tired with all the outpouring of her energy, for her energy was no longer boundless. 10. And she desired to rest, but could not rest. And she spoke to the Snake, saying: Snake, what must I do now? 11. And the Snake said: First daughter of creation, you must go to the Mistress of All Things and ask Her to make the world dark that you may rest. 12. And so she asked that of Her, and She darkened the world for a period that Her daughter might rest. And this was the first night.

13. But when the darkness came, the Snake called to the waters and said: Waters, it is dark once more as it was in the beginning, and now you may come together, and all will be nothingness again. 14. And the waters heard it and began to flood the earth, and many were the creatures destroyed in that flood.

15. But the Mistress of All Things saw this and descended to the earth, placing Her heel upon the head of the Snake and bruising it. 16. And She flung the waters into the air that they might fall harmlessly to the earth in small drops. And this was the first rain.

Chapter Three

AND as the rain fell, the light came again, and a rainbow appeared in the sky, shedding its light upon all things. 2. And whereas all things had been golden, now they took on every hue and colour, and the world was beautiful; but it was not so beautiful as it had formerly been.

3. And She set Her seven Powers in the firmament, giving one to rule each colour of the earth.

4. And She said to Her daughter: what you have done may not be undone, for you have acted with My Spirit, and henceforth shall time be divided into day and night that you may rest. 5. But I shall keep watch in the heavens by night, and there shall be silver light that there may never be complete darkness. 6. By this shall I govern the movements of the waters, that the earth may never again be flooded. 7. The golden light of day will bring all goodness, but it will be too bright for your eyes. The silver light of night, that you may look upon.

8. The Snake shall keep the form that you have given it, and you shall be set in governance over it; but remember that it will ever attempt to beguile and destroy you as it has this night.

9. I shall not live as close to you as before, but still I shall pour blessings upon you, and you may give Me gifts—not in every moment as before, for you have learned to tire, but My light shall give you signs in this matter.

10. And the Mistress of All Things withdrew Herself into the sky, until She seemed but a slender crescent of light. 11. And the first daughter of creation fell to her knees and wept. And these were the first tears shed upon the whole of the earth.

Commentary

IN ITS current form, and in Telluria, this *mythos* would appear to be only about thirty years old, though its roots lie in the oldest Creation myth known in Europe. To Aristasians it represents the primal Creation Story of Aristasia Pura, while by others it is considered the perfect rendition of the Creation for those who love Dea in the late Iron Age.

We shall not give here a verse-by-verse commentary, but shall seek to elucidate a few of the most important elements of the *mythos*.

The Divine Laughter and Dance are the primary elements of creation. While they may seem almost synonymous, they are quite distinct. Laughter has two important functions:

First it shows the creation of the cosmos through the pri-

mary medium of *sound*. Sound is the first of the sensible qualities, connected with Aethyr, which is often called the Fifth
Element, but in terms of Creation is the First Element from
which the other four are born. The concept of the divine female
Voice (*vac*) as the primary cause of creation again goes back to
the earliest Indo-European roots.

Second it indicates the divine *lila* or play. According to traditional doctrine, Creation is first and foremost the Divine Act of
playfulness. Indeed one of the fundamental names of Dea is
Lalita—She Who plays.

The dance, as always, represents order or harmony: *thamë* to
use the Aristasian term. The dance is the Golden Order of the
cosmos. The very word *kosmos* means order, as opposed to *kaos,*
and the Creation is the Divine Act of Ordering, or bringing
cosmos out of chaos.

Order is also the Divine Beauty (hence our word *cosm*etic).
Thus Creation is the imposition of Form and Beauty upon the
blank chaos of non-existence. Beauty and Order, far from being
mere human conceptions, are the very nature of being itself,
without which nothing could exist.

The description of Our Mother as "pure consciousness or
energy", again indicates two distinct things. As the divine Energy, or *Shakti*, the Mother is the Creatrix of all being. She is
not the energy, or power, of a "god" as in later patriarchal traditions, but of Absolute Deity, Dea-Beyond-Form, sometimes
known as the Dark Mother (cf. the Filianic Creed). In the *Devi
Gita* also, Dea is clearly shown as the divine *shakti* or energy,
but not as any form of "consort". She is the Uncaused Cause,
the One without a Second. As one scholar has commented on
the *Devi Gita*, She is "shakti of all and consort of none".

Pure Consciousness (*chit*) is also a frequent designation of Dea
in the *Devi Gita*. She is shown to be the sole Consciousness of the
cosmos, the single Self (*Atma*) of which all lesser selves are but
fragments.

The "Golden Time" when all things were golden should not
be confused with the Golden Age, or first era of worldly history (or of any major historical cycle)—although on a lower

level, the Golden Age(s) do reflect the primordial Golden Time. Rather this "time" is literally "pre-historic"—the time before time itself: the first, perfect Creation. In this time maid saw things, but she saw them only in the light of Dea. She participated in the Divine creativity, taking part in the sacred act of Naming: for just as sound is the origin of Creation, so the primordial Names of things contain their very essences.

The Snake is found in both the Indo-European and Semitic creation myths. The image of the Mother treading on the head of the snake is a part of Christianity, just as it is of the earliest Greek creation story. In some texts, the snake is referred to as "he"—a designation clearly meaningless in Aristasia. In Telluria the snake is sometimes taken as a representative of the masculine principle (thus it is "barren"). The warning that it will "ever attempt to beguile and destroy you" has been seen as the threat of patriarchy. However, this can also be seen as the false self: the tendency in each of us away from Dea and Truth. The two interpretations are not opposed, for every external conflict is but the exteriorization of the deeper internal conflict within the soul.

The nature of the snake is complex. In the first place, it represents *chaos*, the anti-cosmic principle: the revolt against being itself. At the same time it invites maid to rest "among the things that are". It is said that in her lowest state maid sees only things and not Dea, in her intermediate state she sees both things and Dea, in her highest state she sees only Dea—or rather she sees Dea in all things, and all things in the light of Dea. The Snake here is tempting her to see things-in-themselves, outside the light of Dea, and this, of course is an illusion since things truly have their being only in Dea.

Thus there is an ambiguity about the Snake-principle. It is at once opposed to the Creation and yet also tends to supplant Dea in the heart of maid *with* the Creation. In some sense, this might be seen as the opposite ambiguity to the true perspective in which Creation is seen both as an illusion and as the expression of Dea Herself.

There is a Divine anti-cosmic principle, and that is the Dark Mother who will in-breathe all Creation at the Night of Time.

The snake, however is not this divine anti-cosmic principle, but an inverse parody of both sacred worldliness (if we may use that expression) and sacred non-worldliness. The Snake is a contradiction, for all that stands against the Divine is necessarily a contradiction.

From another, and complementary, perspective, the Snake can be seen as the tamasic tendency.

By embracing the Snake, maid falls from the state of Primordial Maid, and the Creation from the state of Primordial Creation. From thence forward the different colours (*varna*) of the world are made manifest. The Powers (or *Janyati*) of Dea are seen as separate from Herself (though that separation is only apparent). The world is no longer golden, representing the direct emanation of pure Light, and both Dea Herself and Her representative, the sun, are now too bright for maid to look upon. The references to the moon prefigure the Daughter, who will mediate that light as Priestess of the World.

The giving of gifts is a reference to the practice of making offerings to Dea: bringing flowers to her shrine; offering up food before we eat it. Some also take it as a reference to the Rite of Sacrifice: the ancient practice of ritually offering bread or honey-cakes to Dea which is mentioned in the Book of Jeremiah and was practiced by the Collyridians in the early centuries of Christianity.

$$\oplus$$

The Mythos of God the Daughter

Authorised Version

Chapter One

WHEN THE FIRST NIGHT had come upon the world, the Mistress of All Things stood alone once more, as She had in the beginning. 2. For a terrible abyss had opened to lie between the world and Her, and Her creatures could not look upon Her brightness.

3. And She stood in contemplation upon the waters of the first darkness; like a great Dove upon the waters She brooded. 4. And She became absorbed within Her and communed with Her own Self; and Her light ceased to shine forth from Her, and yet Her light grew greater. 5. And She fell to Her knees. And the surface of the waters became turbulent, and the great waves curled over Her, and their white foam could not be seen in all that darkness.

6. And when the waters became calm again, the Mistress of All Things rose to Her feet. 7. for She had conceived a Daughter that was not separate from Her, but one with Her, and the child of Her Light.

Chapter Two

AND SHE WALKED across the seas and deep into the forests of the earth until She came upon the deep cave that was at the centre. 2. And She entered the cave. And a star rose above the sacred grove that lay about the cave, brighter and more resplendent than all the stars of the heavens. 3. And the star was seen all over the earth; and the children of the earth were filled with wonder, and they came to the place where the star stood in the sky. 4. And those that were princesses among them brought their crowns to the sacred grove as gifts, and shepherdesses brought the new-dropped lambs, and all the daughters of the earth brought forth the fruits thereof to lay before the cave.

5. But before the cave stood a Janya of Dea, robed in a garment so white that the eyes of earth's children were dazzled, and with a countenance of such great beauty that it was a fearful thing to look upon it. 6. And the daughters of the earth covered their eyes and threw themselves to the ground.

7. And the voice of the Janya was like to the rushing of a thousand waters. 8. And she spoke, saying: Be not afraid, for a new light is dawning over the world. Be not afraid, but approach no further, for if you cannot look on me, how should you look upon my Lady, whose handmaiden I am?

9. And her voice grew gentle, like the wind among the icicles, and sweet beyond all telling. 10. And she spoke, saying: This night shall a Child be born that shall be the Daughter of Light and the Princess of all the world. 11. A Child is coming that shall carry the light of Dea into every part of Creation; even to the most desolate of the places of darkness. 12. Rejoice, poor wanderers of the earth and exiles from the house of your Mother, for to you shall come a Guide and a Deliverer.

13. And when the voice of the Janya ceased, a silence fell that was the first true silence since the beginning of the world, and the last that shall be until it end. 14. And the children of earth watched the sky as the first rays of dawn crept across the heavens.

15. And a cry issued out of the cave, saying:

The holy Child is born from the most holy Mother;
Light has come forth from Light, Perfection from Perfection.

16. And at once the air was filled with the daughters of heaven, and the sky was ablaze with the radiance of their joy. 17. And they sang aloud to the glory of Dea.

18. And when the Shining Ones ceased from their song, the world became quiet again. And the star grew brighter and ever

brighter, until it shone more bright than the radiance of all the host of Heaven; and yet so gentle was its light that the eyes of earth's children were not dazzled. 19. And the colour of the light was not one of the seven, but a wondrous luminance not known within the boundaries of the world.

20. And the Janya at the cave's mouth called forth the children of the earth that they might present their gifts. And the three great princesses of the earth came forward: 21. First the greatest of them, who ruled more land than either of the others and also possessed more treasure. 22. And her crown was of pure gold; and as she took it from her head, the light of the star fell upon it, and it shone with a glister more lovely than any earthly jewel. 23. And she laid it at the feet of the Janya.

24. And the Janya said: It is good that you bring your crown, for you are a great princess, but the Holy Child shall be Princess of all the world.

25. The second princess held neither so much land nor treasure, but she was a maid of deep wisdom and meditation profound. And her crown was of pure silver; and as she took it from her head, the light of the star fell upon it, and it shone with a radiance yet more lovely than that of the golden crown.

26. And she laid it at the feet of the Janya.

27. And the Janya said: It is good that you bring your crown, for you have great wisdom, but the Holy Child is the Daughter of Wisdom Herself.

28. The last princess possessed but few of the world's things, but she was a priestess of Dea, and she praised Her in the morning and at evening and at all the seven hours of the day. And her crown was made from glittering crystal; and as she took it from her head the light of the star fell upon it, and she was bathed in rays of a thousand different hues, and the children of the earth drew in their breath at the sight of its beauty. 29. And she laid it at the feet of the Janya.

30. And the Janya said: It is good that you bring your crown, for you are a true and loving priestess and a servant of your people, but the Holy Child shall be Priestess of all the world, and

shall serve Her children even to the last and greatest service.

31. And when the Janya ceased to speak, a new voice filled the air, more beautiful and more terrible than hers. And it said:

Her Name shall be called Inanna,
For She shall be Lady of Heaven.

32. And the star vanished from the sky and yet its light remained. And the shape of the light became a vision. 33. And the vision was a vision of the Mistress of All Things, bearing in Her arms the Holy Child. 34. And for all the wondrous things the children of earth had seen that night, not the whole of them was one thousandth part as wondrous as this vision.

35. And for twelve nights the star returned to the sky; and on the thirteenth night it did not return. And this was a sign of things that were to come.

Chapter Three

WHEN THE HOLY CHILD had grown to the full stature of maidenhood, the Mother of All Things took Her to a high place upon the earth, saying: To You I give the governance of all these things. 2. You shall command the movements of the waters, and the wind shall be Your servant. 3. The seasons of the earth shall You control, and all the times and seasons in the lives of My creatures. 4. Every soul on earth and in the heavens shall be given into Your care, and the highest stars of the firmament shall know You as their Sovereign. 5. For all these things must be put from Me; for they can no longer look upon My brightness.

6. And the Maid ruled over all the world, making the earth grow fruitful and attending to the prayers of Her creatures, and oftentimes making prayers of Her own that they might come closer to the Mother. 7. And Divine Light shone once more upon the earth, and the Maid was a friend to every creature, and all who turned to Her were filled with life, and with the peace that comes of wholeness.

8. For the waxing and the waning of twelve moons reigned the Maid. 9. And after the twelfth moon had appeared in the sky, the Mother of All Things called Her Daughter to Her, and spoke to Her, saying: You have made the whole earth fruitful and brought My light to all the world, have You not satisfaction in Your work?

10. And the Maid replied, saying: I have brought Your light to many places, and yet a place there is that remains ever in darkness; a place beneath all places, in which there is no light. 11. And the ways of entrance to that place are many, for there is a place at the bottom of each earthly soul into which Your light cannot shine.

12. And Her Mother asked of Her: Do You know what thing it is that You must do if You will bring My light into every place?

13. And the Maid replied: I know what it is that I must do.

14. For She knew that She must descend into the nether regions, giving up the Divine light and going down into that place wherein is no light, but only the profoundest darkness.

15. And this was Her taking on of fate upon Herself.

16. And the Mother of All things removed the Divine light from Her Daughter, and blessing Her, sent Her forth, saying: Go hence from here, beloved Daughter, for You may no longer look upon Me.

17. And the Children of Heaven led Her forth, and praised Her in strange and gentle songs. 18. And the Maid set Herself apart to pray, and She prayed alone by the running streams and beneath the full moon, until a new light was kindled within Her, which was the pure light of Her own divinity. 19. Yet while the divine light of Her Mother was undying, the light of the Maid trembled before the winds of death.

20. And the daughters of Heaven delighted in Her gentle light, saying: This trembling light is the glory of all the heavens, and more glorious than all the luminaries thereof.

21. And the Maid answered them, saying: I shall carry this light into every place that is, even into the nethermost regions and the regions of death.

22. And they led Her forth and clothed Her in the white robe of the sacrifice.

Chapter Four

THE MAID took up the great Moon-Axe, whose silver blades were as the crescents of the moon, in symbol of Her light, and went alone into a desert place. 2. And, knowing that She had not the light of Her Mother upon Her, malefic demons gathered about and beset Her; demons of fear and of dread isolation, and every sort of restriction. 3. And they tore Her soul with their talons, crying: Hope is dead, for the light of the Mother is fallen from You. 4. You shall go down to suffering and death and none shall save You. In the illimitable emptiness of the universe shall You stand alone and none shall give You comfort. 5. In the darkness of eternal night shall You kneel to weep and no hand shall be put upon Your shoulder, but every hand shall be raised against You to do you hurt.

6. And the Maid was filled with trembling, but She answered: Go your ways, for what I have said, that shall I do.

7. And the demons spoke, saying: Be You led by us, and You shall have protection and all good things. 8. The whole of the world shall be Your fortress, and You shall have wealth and magnificence that all the children of the earth shall love You.

9. But the Maid answered: How shall you give to Me that which is Mine? 10. For I am the Princess of the world, and all the children of the earth have been given into My care by the hand of the Eternal.

11. Then the demons said: The light of the Eternal is taken from You, and whether these things are or are not Yours, it is we that that have the power of them, and we that You must obey if You will be saved.

12. But the Maid replied, saying: That which is right in the deepest heart of things, and in the centre of all being, that is right and none other; and the Truth alone is true. 13. Nor shall all the powers of the earth count against it, neither all the powers of the seas and the skies move it by the smallest fraction in all its vastness. 14. I shall obey none but My Mother, though all

your power be turned in fury upon Me.

15. And the demons cried: Not our power, but the power of one far greater from whom our power derives.

16. And the Maid said: Thus may it be.

17. And the demons questioned Her, saying: Think You that Your Mother will save You?

18. And the Maid answered: She will do what She will do, and blessed is Her Name.

19. And the demons laughed, saying: Then are You abandoned to the uttermost darkness.

20. And the heart of the Maid fainted within Her.

21. And She said: Thus may it be.

Chapter Five

AND THE MAID journeyed down into the darkest regions until She came to the great gates of the Nether World. 2. And the gatekeeper cried: Who is it that comes of her own free step upon the realm of the Dark Queen? 3. And the Maid replied: I am the Daughter of She Who is Mother of all.

4. And the gatekeeper said: Give me your axe, and You may pass. And the Maid gave the great Moon-Axe into her hands, and the vast oaken gate swung open that She might pass through.

5. And the Maid came to a second gate, and was again halted by the keeper thereof. And the gatekeeper said: Give me the circlet from Your head, and You may pass. 6. And the Maid gave the silver circlet into her hands and passed through the gate.

7. And She came to a third gate, and the gatekeeper said: Give me Your white linen headdress and You may pass. And She did this and passed bareheaded through the gate.

8. And She came to a fourth gate, and the gatekeeper said: Give me Your blue cloak and You may pass. And She gave Her blue cloak into the hands of the gatekeeper, and passed through the gate.

9. And She came to a fifth gate and the gatekeeper said:

Give me your sandals and You may pass. And She unlaced Her sandals and passed barefooted through the gate.

10. And She came to a sixth gate, and the gatekeeper said: Give me the silver girdle about Your waist and You may pass. And She unbound Her silver girdle and passed through the gate wearing only Her white robe.

11. And She came to a seventh gate, and the gatekeeper said: Give me your hair and You may pass. And She bowed Her head, and Her hair was shorn from Her, and She passed into the chamber of the Dark Queen.

12. And the Dark Queen spoke, saying: Are You the Princess of the world, and the Daughter of She Who is Mother of all? And the Maid replied: I am She.

13. And Her hands were bound, and the daughters of the Dark Queen taunted Her and beat Her, and pulled Her short hair. And She was dragged to Her knees before the Dark Queen.

14. And the Dark Queen rose to her feet, and so terrible was her aspect that her daughters fled to the furthest part of the chamber. 15. And she turned her eyes upon the Maid, that have been beheld by no creature of the upper world. For her eyes are the eyes of death. 16. And the Maid, looking upon her eyes, became a lifeless corse and a dead thing upon the ground.

17. And at the centre of the Nether World there stood a great pillar, reaching to the roof of that world. 18. And the daughters of the Dark Queen took the corse of the Maid, and hung it high upon that pillar. 19. And above Her head they hung the great Moon-Axe, in symbol of the greatness of the deed.

Chapter Six

NOW FROM THE TIME when the Daughter of Heaven had passed through the first gate of Hell, a barrenness had fallen on the earth; and neither bird had sung nor any flower showed its beauty forth; nor was there joy in any heart. 2. But when the Maid was slain upon the pillar of the world, an awful darkness fell on all the earth. 3. And the rivers of the earth ceased to flow, but drained away into the salt sea, and the sea ceased to move, but stood still in awful stagnancy. 4. And there was drouth in all the earth. And neither maid bore child nor ewe brought forth the lamb. And every growing thing began to wither from its roots. 5. And in the nights were neither moon nor stars, and the heat of the sun by day was terrible.

6. And the Mother of All Things wept and walked in sorrow over earth and Heaven.

7. And the children of the earth prayed to Her, weeping for the world and for Her Daughter. 8. And in the darkness after the second day, a star appeared in the heavens, whose brightness was too great for them to look upon.

9. And the children of earth rejoiced, saying: It is the Mistress of All Things, come to seek Her Daughter. And the Dark Queen ordered the gates of Hell to be shut and barred against Her.

10. And the gatekeeper stood within the gate, and cried: Who is it that comes upon the realm of the Dark Queen? And She answered, saying: I am the Mistress of all that is, and the Mother of My Daughter. 12. Give Me entrance, for if you give Me not entrance, I will smash the bolt and shatter the gatepost. I will raise up the great gate of Hell and break it asunder.

13. But the gatekeeper opened not the gate. And the Mistress of All Things clapped Her hands together, so that the whole world shook, and the great gate of Hell was shattered in fragments, and the nether regions trembled to the very foundations. 14. And the gatekeeper covered her eyes and fled, for she could not look upon the brightness of the Mistress of All Things.

15. And the Mistress of All Things came into the Nether World; and the six gatekeepers flung wide their gates and fled.

16. And Her Janyati took down the corse of Her Daughter, and laid it upon Her knees; and She wept anew, for none but She could know the awful depth of the oblivion in which Her Daughter lay. And She sprinkled on the corse the water of Life, which She had gathered from the holy tears of Her own sor-

row. 17. And Her Daughter rose again and was alive again. 18. And amid tears of joy, They embraced and were one. And after this, the Daughter stood alone. 19. And the souls of the Nether World were awakened by Her gentle light, and followed Her through the shattered gates of Hell.

20. And when they beheld Her, the children of the earth rejoiced, and the rivers flowed again, and the sea began to move.

21. And the children of the earth cried: lift up your voices in song and laughter, for the Princess of the World was dead and is alive again, was broken and is whole; and there is no place whereto Her joyous rule does not extend. 22. Give praise to the Mother of All Things and praise to Her Daughter.

23. Rejoice, for the world is renewed.

Chapter Seven

AND AS SHE WALKED, the children of the earth threw blossoms before Her, and though Her feet rested on them, yet they were not bruised. 2. And She reigned over all the earth, bringing all nature back to life, and all life back to the true law and rhythm of nature. And the whole world knew Her as its Princess. 3. And the children of the earth were filled with love for Her, and gathered about Her with tears of joy, touching Her robes and giving themselves to Her in their hearts. 4. And She gathered them together and taught them many things, saying: You have gained knowledge of the world, but I say, be not wise with the wisdom of the world, nor proud with the pride of the world, nor strait with the dignity of the world, neither lose your self in any of the ways and fashions of the world, but come to Me as little children in the pure simplicity of your hearts and the virgin innocence of your souls—for truly, all of you are children in the eyes of your Mother, and I shall receive all who come as Her children. Come you so to Me and all faults shall be forgiven. And She showed them how to offer Sacrifice to the Mother of All Things.

5. And She said: When the time is come for Me to go from

you, still I shall be with you and shall never leave you, not for one fragment of an hour until we are together in completion. 6. But I shall unite you all who love Me in one great body; 7. The highest and the lowest, the living and the dead, those who falter at the door, and those who have climbed to the highest tower, all shall be one in My body which I have given to the world, and all shall be nourished by My Spirit.

8. And they understood Her not, but only wept that She must leave them. And She spoke no more of this, but taught them, and revealed many hidden things, such as might fill an hundred books.

9. And when the time was at hand, two Janyati descended, one on either side of Her, and She went with them into Heaven.

10. And the children of Heaven greeted Her, crying: Hail, Princess of the World; Hail, Queen of Heaven. And they placed a crown of stars about Her head. 11. And the blue night was Her cloak, and the stars of the sky the crown about Her head, and the moon lay at Her feet. And they cried again: Hail, Queen of Heaven.

12. And thus began Her dear and glorious reign. And for the children of Heaven, Her very Presence was the completion of their joy. 13. And She poured forth Her grace and blessing from Her hands upon them and upon the earth. And Her grace and blessing were as rays of perfect Light which penetrate the heart and flood the soul.

14. And She said to them: Do not forget your sisters of the earth, but move yourselves among them and hear their voices; lend them succour and breathe with them in their upward aspiration. 15. And when a soul in true devotion passes from the earth, lead her to the portal of Heaven and the garden of Avala, and give her rest, and provision her with treasures of the Spirit to help her on her way.

16. And She entered the great Temple of Heaven, where the spirits of earth's children were gathered at the Sacrifice, even as their souls were gathered on the earth.

17. And She stood at the great Altar and took up a wheaten

loaf, and spoke, saying: 18. Like to the corn, My body was cut down by the scythe of death; and like to the corn did it rise anew. 19. For I am the ear of corn that is reaped in silence.

20. And She said: Like to the grain was my body broken between the stones of death. And saying thus, She broke the bread between Her hands.

21. And She gave the fragments of the bread to the spirits of earth's children, saying: Here is My body that is broken for you. Eat My body, that you may be one with My body, and may be one body in Me.

22. And She poured out Her Spirit from Her hands into a great chalice, and Her Spirit lay as wine within the chalice. And She said: Even as you have offered Me bread in Sacrifice, so I give you the bread of My body; and as you have poured out libations of wine to Me, so I pour out the eternal libation of My eternal Spirit.

24. And as it is performed above in the Spirit, so is it reflected below in the body and the soul, and through the reflection do earth's children have part in the Real. 25. And so were the things that are told in this book reflected in the hearts of maids, that all might read them and draw closer to She that acted them.

NOTE: It has been argued by some that the final ten verses of the Daughter Mythos as presented here are not part of the original. They appear to imply a Collyridian-style Communion Service, perhaps combined with an Offering of bread and wine. The language also has something in common with the Eleusinian Mysteries of Demeter (Dea-Mater, Mother God) and Her Daughter Persephone, also known as Kore ("the Maid"). Devotees may regard these verses as deuterocanonical if they prefer to do so.

Part II
SANSKRIT TEXTS

THE SECOND part of this book presents Sanskrit texts. These are important because they come out of a Tradition that descends seamlessly from the earliest times. Certainly it has been subject to patriarchal redaction and re-interpretation, but it has no historical "founder" or starting-point.

Adaptations of the Indian tradition were made both to patriarchy and, more broadly, to the changed mentality of Kali Yuga, but these were not "revolutionary" changes.

One effect of this was that the Universal Religion of Our Mother God, so clearly the sole faith of the early Indus Valley civilisation (as of all other early civilisations), was never "officially repudiated" (compare the fulminations of the prophet Jeremiah against the women of Jerusalem for holding Divine Service to the Queen of Heaven).

Thus, during the Mediaeval period, the worship of the Supreme Dea was able to return in an absolute thealogical form, and Our Mother God could be proclaimed once again the supreme and only Deity.

Naturally, this thealogical revival took place within a patriarchal society, but it gave rise to some texts that are absolutely orthodox from a Déanic point of view as well as being part of an unbroken tradition going back to the earliest pre-patriarchal times.

We are also able to see the thealogical unity between the statements of this revival of the Primordial Tradition and Déanic/Filianic faith as we know and practise it.

Our Sanskrit texts come from two thealogical sources:

1. Texts of the Déanic Revival already discussed.

2. Thea-philosophical texts in which the patriarchal element is inessential and in which a linguistic adaptation to feminine faith is natural and legitimate in the light of 1. above. To illustrate this category, we include an adaptation of the Isa Upanishad.

39

The Great Hymn to Mahalakshmi

O Mahalakshmi I salute Thee,
Thou art Mahamaya and Sripitha,
Worshipped art thou by angels
Holder of conch, disc and mace,
O Mahalakshmi I salute Thee.

O Mahalakshmi I salute thee,
Mounted art thou on the back of Garuda,
Thou art a terror most formidable to Asura Kola,
Thou removest all sins,
O Dea, Mahalakshmi, obeisance to Thee.

Mahalakshmi, thou knowest all.
Giver of boons art thou to all,
Formidable destroyer of all evil,
Remover of all pain and sorrow,
Mahalakshmi, salutation to Thee.

O Dea, Mahalakshmi,
Thou art the Giver of Intelligence and success
And of both worldly enjoyment and Liberation
Thou art the self of mantra,
O Mahalakshmi, obeisance to Thee.

Thou art without beginning or end,
O supreme Dea, Mahalakshmi,
Thou art the primaeval Power and art born of yoga
Mahalakshmi, salutation to Thee.

Thou art both gross and subtle
Thou art terrible and a great power,
Thou removest all great sins,
O Mahalakshmi obeisance to Thee.

O Dea enthroned on the lotus,
Thou art the supreme Brahman,
The ever-pervading Atman,
Thou art the great Raya and Mother of the world,
O Dea, salutation to Thee.

O Dea, clad in white raiment,
Adorned with varied gems,
Mother and Upholder of the world art Thou,
Mahalakshmi, obeisance to Thee.

Commentary

With the exception of a few minor changes (such as Dea for Devi) this is the Avalon translation made very early in the 20th century. The hymn itself is of great antiquity, probably long predating its first written form in the *Padma* (Lotus) *Purana*, which Western scholarship (which tends to err considerably toward late datings owing to certain prejudices inherent in its methods) places between 400. and 1000. A.D.

Certain benefits are traditionally associated with this hymn:

> *Whoever with devotion reads this hymn to Mahalak-shmi, composed in eight stanzas, attains all success through the Grace of Mahalakshmi.*
>
> *Whoever reads this hymn at least once a day will have all her sins destroyed*.*
>
> *She who recites it twice will be blessed with wealth and prosperity.*
>
> *She who recites this three times in a day will have all obstacles destroyed* and be free from all enmity and harm. She will be always be blessed by Dea Mahalakshmi.*
>
> *Let Great Lakshmi manifest in us with all Her beautiful and nourishing qualities.*

* Sometimes rendered as "the Great Enemy (ego) will be destroyed". The two readings are not opposed, as the phrase has both a material and a spiritual sense.

Commentaries on the Verses

**O Mahalakshmi I salute Thee,
Thou art Mahamaya and Sripitha,
Worshipped art thou by angels
Holder of conch, disc and mace,
O Mahalakshmi I salute Thee.**

Sri Mahalakshmi is both **Mahamaya**—the creatrix of all material and non-material manifestation—and **Sripitha**, the sacred abode, the dwelling at the very heart of being, the Realm of God that is "within you". Thus Sri Mahalakshmi, as the manifestation of Dea Herself, represents both the infinitely great and extended, and the infinitely small and central.

Following our usual practice, we translate "Devas" here as **Angels**, this being the most accurate rendering in Western terminology.

Conch, Disc and Mace are the attributes held in three of Her four hands (the fourth would normally hold a lotus). In other iconography She is depicted as holding lotuses in her two upper hands, and pouring a shower of gold from one of the lower ones while extending the fourth in a gesture of blessing.

The **Conch** is the fountain that produces the five elements: first aethyr and from that the four material elements: air, fire, water and earth in that order. The conch is associated with the Primordial Sound from which all manifestation proceeds. It should be noted here that the primordial element of aethyr is associated with sound and, in the human microcosm, with the sense of hearing.

The Conch is held in Her lower right hand which represents the revolving or creative tendency. We may note here the very fundamental Indo-European root *wert* which means both turning and becoming and gives rise to all our *ver* "turning" words (reverse, transverse, vertigo, vortex etc.) as well as German werdë*ns* (=becoming), also weird (=fate), worthy (=wellbecome, or "becoming") and the Aristasian word werdë, which means "fate" in the sense of *karma* (using that word in the

42

modern Western, rather than the fuller Indian understanding of the term*).

The full study of this word-group would provide a fascinating insight into the metaphysical bases of our language, which itself derives from the Primordial Sound ("verse" is also part of this group, and "word"—from the Indo-European root *werdh a word, from *wer, to speak, which also gives rise to Latin *verbum* and "word" words in most Indo-European languages—while not directly related is closely connected in symbolic linguistics). All these conceptions are inherent in the Conch held in Sri Lakshmi's lower right hand.

The **Disc** (or Chakra) has six spokes. It represents the limitless mistressship of the six directions of space. It is held in the upper right hand, which represents the cohesive tendency. The Disc, shining like a child-sun, represents the mind. It is also a formidable weapon which decapitates the demons and thus belongs secondarily to the Vikhelic and protective nature of Dea.

The **Mace** represents the elemental force from which all physical and mental powers are derived. It is held in the lower left hand which represents the idea of individual existence. It is also representative of cosmic Intellect or knowledge. A further association of the Mace is with time and thus also with Kali, the power of time.

O Mahalakshmi I salute thee,
Mounted art thou on the back of Garuda,
Thou art a terror most formidable to Asura Kola,
Thou removest all sins,
O Dea Mahalakshmi, obeisance to Thee,

Garuda is the great Bird (depicted sometimes as an eagle, sometimes as an owl). Sri Lakshmi's seat thereon indicates her transcendence of the material world and is also seen as the vantage-point from which She rescues Her devotees from the

* The western usage of the term *karma*, which is influenced by pop-Buddhism, is a valid concept, but not an accurate interpretation of the word in most traditional contexts. Aristasian werdë thus supplies a useful term to our language.

43

turbulent ocean of Samsara. Garuda is also a warlike creature thus emphasising again the Vikhelic nature.

Sri Lakshmi is the destroyer of the demon (*asura*) Kola, who is the symbol of ignorance. Thus her defeat of the demon, while mythologically represented as a single event, is in fact a continuing reality. Ignorance here is especially that ignorance (*avidya*) that keeps us ensnared in the illusion of Samsara. We must understand that Vikhelic, or warlike, symbology, while it may have literal protective qualities against the actual dark forces of the cosmos, also refers to the struggle against what is imperfect in ourselves.

Mahalakshmi, thou knowest all.
Giver of boons art thou to all,
Formidable destroyer of all evil,
Remover of all pain and sorrow,
Mahalakshmi, salutation to Thee.

Giver of boons art thou to all … Remover of all pain and sorrow: Mahalakshmi, who combines the qualities of Sai Thamë (the Great Benefic and Ruler of the Golden Order) and Sai Sushuri (the embodiment of Divine Love), grants boons to Her devotees and removes pain and sorrow, freeing them from the bonds of sin.

Formidable destroyer of all evil: Nonetheless, the Vikhelic quality, symbolised by Her **Disc**, is never forgotten in the Indian tradition, where the resurgence of the worship of Dea in the Kali Yuga (or Age of Iron) centred initially about her warrior-forms and the epic battles in which She single-handedly destroyed the great demons that the "gods" could not defeat.

This is because of the Vikhelic quality of the Iron Age, in which the true nature of Supreme Dea is easily eclipsed by patriarchal forms. If Dea is to be worshipped as the sole and supreme Deity, as She was in the beginning, without attributing some of Her Qualities to masculine forms, then She must manifest Her warrior Qualities to defend Her devotees from the dark forces rampant in an Age of Iron.

O Dea, Mahalakshmi,
Thou Art the Giver of Intelligence and success
And of both worldly enjoyment and Liberation
Thou at the self of mantra,
O Mahalakshmi, obeisance to Thee.

The parallelism of the second and third lines could be lost upon a modern reader, who would be inclined to read **Intelligence success** and **worldly enjoyment** as three broadly material goods and **Liberation** as the only spiritual one. Actually they are two matched pairs for Intelligence, in traditional thought, does not mean mere worldly reason, but that transcendent faculty by which we grasp the fundamental Realities behind worldly existence (and which is thus the necessary precursor to reason). Reason is the lunar reflection of the Solar Intelligence. Thus we have an example of what is called *chiastic* (or X-shaped) *parallelism*:

Intelligence and **Liberation** (from worldly attachments) belong together, as do **success** and **worldly enjoyment**. The importance of this verse is its indication of the balance between worldly and spiritual goods offered by Mahalakshmi. Worldly people pursue only the things of this world. Spiritual ascetics preach a complete abstinence from the world. Worshipping our bounteous Lady, we may combine the two—innocent worldly pleasure and spiritual advancement.

The statement **Thou Art the self of mantra** must be understood in the light of the doctrine that a mantra, being a representation of one of the cardinal modifications of the Primordial

Sound, embodies the Deity Herself.

**Thou Art without beginning or end,
O supreme Dea, Mahalakshmi,
Thou art the primaeval Power and art born of yoga
Mahalakshmi, salutation to Thee.**

Thou Art without beginning or end makes it clear that Dea predates the Universe and time itself. She is the causeless Cause, "the unoriginated Origin of being". All things that are must have a beginning and an end; and ultimately, all things begin in Dea and end in Her. Only She is without beginning and without end.

Thou art ... born of yoga clearly does not mean that Dea originates in any human practice, for it has already been stated that she has no beginning and no end; while yoga itself (meaning literally "union") is only the joining of the human soul to Dea. A less poetic translation puts these lines thus: "*She is the divine fire (Cosmic will) of the all yogas and she dawns in the minds of yogis*". In other words, it is through the yoga of devotion (*bhakti yoga*) and other spiritual practices that we may experience Her actual presence.

**Thou art both gross and subtle,
Thou art terrible and a great power,
Thou removest all great sins,
O Mahalakshmi obeisance to Thee.**

Both gross and subtle indicates that Dea manifests herself in both "gross" (apparent-bodily) form and in Her subtle (formless) state. She rules both the material world and all the subtle degrees of manifestation.

The word **terrible** (perhaps confusing because of its colloquial usage) is also applied to the Christian vision of Deity. It indicates the "holy terror" felt by beings when confronted with the awesome majesty of supreme Deity. The *Devi Gita* describes the awe and terror felt by the angels when faced with Dea in Her unmodified majesty; whereupon She graciously showed Herself in Her beautiful apparent-bodily form in order to reassure and comfort them.

O Dea enthroned on the lotus,
Thou art the supreme Brahman,
The ever-pervading Atman,
Thou art the great Raya and Mother of the world,
O Dea, salutation to Thee.

The **Lotus** (which is also the fourth Attribute, with **Conch**, **Disc** and **Mace**) represents the flowering of manifestation, unfolding upon the waters of the *prima materia* or unformed matter. Dea, either standing in the form of the Vertical Ray, or seated in meditation, represents the Essence which gives form to substance or *materia* and allows the lotus of manifestation to blossom into all its multifoliate variety.

Thou art the supreme Brahman/The ever-pervading Atman. She is both Transcendent Deity and Immanent Deity. Supreme Brahman is the highest expression of Deity, while Atman means both "breath" and "Spirit"—as does Latin *Spiritus* (cf. "respiration"), Greek *pneuma* and Hebrew *ruach*—it is the Divine Breath that breathes in every creature, it is the true Self of all beings, which is not other than Dea Herself.

Great Raya and Mother of the world represents a difficult translation problem. Such words as *Ishwari* and *Jaganmaadhaah* mean Lord in the feminine. There is no English equivalent. In Aristasia, the word *Raya* means "Lady" in the "Lord" sense and is undoubtedly be the best translation if one is willing not to adhere to "standard" English.

O Dea, clothed in white raiment,
Adorned with varied gems,
Mother and Upholder of the world art Thou,
Mahalakshmi, obeisance to Thee.

Clothed in white raiment represents the pure, undifferentiated Deity beyond form, while **adorned with varied gems** represents all the various and beautiful forms of Her creation.

Once again the balance between worldly fecundity and variety on the one hand and spiritual purity and oneness on the other is expressed. Here the gems, adorning Dea Herself, represent manifest variety in its purest form: the Celestial Archetypes as they proceed directly from Dea, represented as precious stones, pure points of unsullied colour; just as the colours of the rainbow are the primary differentiations of the original pure white light. The primary forms of these gems or pure colours are the seven Great Janyati.

Mother and upholder of the world art Thou: Just as Dea has created the world, so she sustains it in every moment of its existence, else it would instantly cease to be.

Thus the hymn ends with a paean to Dea as the supporter of life and creation, balancing Her undifferentiated Transcendent nature and Her creative Beauty in its highest and purest aspect —which is that aspect closest to Her.

In this last stanza, the devotee is symbolically caught up in the arms of Dea, or rather, is invited to realise that she has never left Her arms, upon whose support she depends for her very existence. Only let us realise the true nature of that endless maternal embrace, and our lives shall become blissful.

$\oplus$

The Angelic Hymn to Dea

From the Devi Gita: an Indian Scripture dating from the 13th-16th centuries that sets forth for the later Kali Yuga the Eternal worship of Dea. It is the feminine equivalent to the Bhagavad Gita.

The Angels (devas), having seen Dea in Her supernal form, salute Her as the Supreme Being.

Hail Dea! Hail Great Dea! Hail forever most auspicious Dea!

Propitious Lady of all Nature, we prostrate ourselves to Thee forever.

O Mother! Thou art the colour of fire; blazing like the Sun with the Light of Wisdom. As pure consciousness Thou shinest everywhere, and art worshipped for the fruits of action.

We take refuge in Thee, O Durga. Hail to thee O Dea, Who art the Barque of Swift Crossing.

The angels created Speech which pervades all things, and whereby all creatures speak.

Most comely is this Speech: a Heavenly Cow yielding food and all desires. Through her do we praise You. May she dwell ever among us.

O Dea, Thou art the Night of Destruction at the world's end, worshipped by Brahma. Thou art Vaisnavi, Thou art the Mother of Skanda, Thou art Sarasvati, Thou art Aditi, Thou art the Daughter of Daksha. Thou dost purify the world in Thy many forms. We bow down to Thee.

We know Thee to be Mahalakshmi, we meditate on Thee as the underlying Power of all things.

O Mother, shed Thy light on us, that we may know Thee through meditation.

O Dea! Obeisance to Thee in the shining order of the world-body; obeisance to Thee in the subtle thread of the world-spirit.

Obeisance to thee in the Unmanifest State; obeisance to thee in the glorious form of Absolute Deity.

Through Thy power of nescience doth the world appear, like to a rope appearing as a serpent or as a garland of flowers.

Through Thy power of Knowledge Thou dissolvest the world back into thine own Self. Glory unto Thee, the Empress of the Universe.

We glorify Her, Who is pure consciousness and whose essence is *That*.

Whose being is Bliss unmelded, Whom all the Scriptures know as their final goal.

Thou transcendest the five bodies. Thou art the Witness of the three states of consciousness.

Thou art the essence of the fragmentary soul, known by the name of *thou*.

O Mother! Hail to Thee who art OM, the primordial Word. Hail to Thee Who pervadest all as HRIM.

Hail to thee, Mother of all sacred sounds. All-compassionate Mother, we bow down at Thy lotus feet.

COMMENTARIES

Hail Dea! Hail Great Dea! Hail forever most auspicious Dea! Propitious Lady of all Nature, we prostrate ourselves to Thee forever.

Commentary

Hail Dea!

We render "Devi" here as Dea, for the word means simply God Who Is Our Mother. The term "Goddess" is misleading, implying something secondary to a male "God", or one of a multiplicity of divinities. Here we are referring to Supreme Deity.

Propitious Lady of all Nature.

"Nature" (*prakriti*) is an aspect, or power, of Dea. It does not refer to insensate matter, but to the Divine Reality that lies behind all manifest being. Nor is this a question of "nature worship" according to the modern misunderstanding of the term, but a recognition that all nature springs from Dea.

O Mother! Thou art the colour of fire; blazing like the Sun with the Light of Wisdom. As pure consciousness Thou shinest everywhere, and art worshipped for the fruits of action.

We take refuge in Thee, O Durga. Hail to thee O Dea, Who art the Barque of Swift Crossing.

Commentary

O Mother! Thou art the colour of fire; blazing like the Sun with the Light of Wisdom.

Our Mother burns like the Sun, for She is the pure light of Wisdom (cf. Greek *Sophia*). She is not a "lunar goddess" but is often depicted in Solar terms.

As pure consciousness Thou shinest everywhere, and art worshipped for the fruits of action.

51

Although She represents the highest Wisdom, attained by strict asceticism, she also is the provider of the fruits of all worldly actions and, because of her loving kindness, she grants those fruits to those who worship Her, both human maids and angels. Pure Consciousness (*Chaitanya*) is a concept closely related to the Divine Act of the creation and sustaining of the Universe. The Pure Consciousness of Dea pervades the universe. She is Ultimately the only Consciousness, of which our lesser consciousnesses are but fragments.

As it is written in another of Her Scriptures, the *Tripura Rahasya* (Mystery of Threefold Dea):

That which shines as "Is" is Her Majesty the Absolute Consciousness. Thus the universe is only the Self—the One and one only.

Tripura Rahasya XI, 85

And again:

Absolute Being, the One Queen, Parameswari (Transcendental Lady) overwhelming the three states and hence called Tripura. Though She is undivided the whole universe manifests in all its variety in Her, being reflected, as it were, in a self-luminous mirror. The reflection cannot be apart from the mirror and is therefore one with it. Such being the case, there cannot be difference in degrees. Bodies are mere conceptions in the lower order of beings and they are not to the point in the case of God. Therefore, be wise, and worship the one pure, unblemished Transcendence.

Tripura Rahasya VII, 93

(Translation of Swami Sri Ramananda Saraswathi)

We take refuge in Thee, O Durga. Hail to thee O Dea, Who art the Barque of Swift Crossing.

She is the sure refuge of the soul. Even the angels take refuge in Her. In seeking Her protection, they may run to Her warlike form of Durga (Vikhë), the great Protectress and Destroyer of Evil. The image of the vessel that brings the soul to the "nether shore" may be found in many traditions. Taking refuge in Dea, we allow Her to conduct us safely over the turbulent ocean of this world, the storm-tossed sea of werdë (*samsara*).

The angels created Speech which pervades all things, and whereby all creatures speak.

Most comely is this Speech: a Heavenly Cow yielding food and all desires. Through her do we praise You. May she dwell ever among us.

Commentary

The Angels created Speech which pervades all things, and whereby all creatures speak.

According to the modernist doctrine, speech "evolved" from animal squeaks and grunts. Yet a study of language teaches us that the earliest languages are the most complex and expressive, while the latest ones are the simplest. Language is continually simplified for the lesser minds of the Age of Iron (Kali Yuga). Even as this Age progresses, language is continually "scaled down". So modern Italian is a much simpler language than Latin.

Where, then, does language come from? Tradition teaches us that it proceeds from the single Word, in which all speech and all being is immanently contained. In the sacred language of Sanskrit, this single Word is represented in our earthly speech by the sacred monosyllable OM, or by the seed-mantra sacred to Dea, HRIM.

This truth is perhaps best known to Filianists from the words of *The Pillar of Light* which are taken as the basic premise of the Aristasian science of linguistics:

> *3. What is your language of the earth, My children? What are the words of thy speech? 4. Are they not fallen from the first, the mother language? Are they not broken and impaired?*

Most comely is this Speech: a Heavenly Cow yielding food and all desires. Through Her do we praise You. May She dwell ever among us.

From the single Divine Word grows the first language, the Language of the Angels. Thus we are told that the Angels created speech. But speech (*Vac*), in the earliest Vedic literatures, is

Herself known as a Form of Dea. She is the all-pervading cosmogonic (world-creating) Deity. Vac is associated with the cow, which represents the nourishing Mother, the Source of all good things*. Thus Speech, in Her highest aspect, is a manifestation of Dea Herself.

The Language of the Angels passed to maids upon earth, and in the earliest days our human speech was very pure, very close to the Angelic Language. But as the Age of Gold gave place to the Age of Silver, and the Age of Silver to the Age of Bronze, so human speech became less perfect, less an instrument for expressing pure Truth. At last there came a time when the Primordial Language was broken into different tongues—at first only a few, representing the major divisions of humanity, and then each of these languages split into various increasingly simplified sub-dialects, until we have the multiplicity of languages that we find today. This is the meaning of the Biblical story of the Tower of Babel.

Thus it is said that the Angels created Speech, but also that Speech, in Her purest essence, is an aspect of Dea that transcends even the Angels. Ultimately, it is only through Dea (in Her form as Speech) that we praise Dea.

---

* Curiously, some scholarly Western commentators have expressed surprise at this maternal, cow-related aspect of Vac in addition to Her grander "cosmic" nature, but the name is clearly related to Latin *vacca*, a cow (French *vache*) as well as to *vox*, voice etc.

The cosmogonic nature of Speech—the association of Speech with the world-creating Power—is clear in the light of the metaphysical link between the naming of things and their creation. The names of things are not mere arbitrary "signs", ultimately evolved from animal noises, but contain, in the Primordial Language, the real Essences of those things. Thus in Sanskrit we have the distinction between *nama* and *rupa: nama* being the name of a thing —its Angelic or primordial Name, and hence its Archetype or real Essence—and *rupa*, or shape, being its outward or worldly manifestation. In a sacred language like Sanskrit, which still retains unbroken links to the Primordial Language, certain names or mantras contain the essence of that which they name. Hence, most obviously, the importance of the Primordial Words OM and HRIM, but also many other words and mantras.

The importance of words and of the Primordial Word (*Logos*) was understood by classical Greek philosophy and passed into Christian thought (note the opening of the Gospel according to St. John). However, both Greek and

O Dea, Thou art the Night of Destruction at the world's end, worshipped by Brahma. Thou art Vaisnavi, Thou art the Mother of Skanda, Thou art Sarasvati, Thou art Aditi, Thou art the Daughter of Daksha. Thou dost purify the world in Thy many forms. We bow down to Thee.

Commentary

O Dea, Thou art the Night of Destruction at the world's end, worshipped by Brahma.

Even as the Mother creates the world at its beginning, so also she breathes it back into Herself at the end; for the worlds in truth were never any other than She. In this aspect, the Devi of the Angelic Hymn represents the Dark Mother of the Filianic Trinity.

Thou art Vaisnavi, Thou art the Mother of Skanda, Thou art Saraswati,

Vaisnavi, the Mother of Skanda and Saraswati represent, in this context, the *Trimurti*—Creator, Sustainer and Destroyer of the Universe, represented in the patriarchal Hindu tradition as Brahma, Vishnu and Shiva. While the Forms of Devi are said in this tradition to be "consorts" of the three male deities, in the true tradition of Dea, She represents in Herself the three aspects of Deity.

In Filianic terms, the Mother is the Creatrix, the Daughter the Preserver and the Dark Mother the Destroyer of the worlds.

Thou art Aditi,

Aditi is a very ancient name of Dea. The name means unfettered or limitless, characteristic of the Cosmic Sky-Deity, though it also has Solar connotations. The Vedas hint that She

---

Latin had already ceased to be true Sacred Languages, even though Latin functioned as an ecclesiastical language in the West.

In the Filianic calendar, the name of the eighth month, Voiś (pron. Voish and corresponding roughly to October), means both speech and butter.

was once recognised as Supreme and is still the Mother of all gods or angels. She is undoubtedly pre-Vedic in origin. The *Devi Gita* continues the thread of this ancient tradition, affirming the supremacy of Dea.

Thou art the Daughter of Daksha.

The Daughter of Daksha, Sati, is an Avatar of Dea. Her story is told in many forms, all surviving ones being patriarchal (and, indeed, forming the basis for the cruel patriarchal practice of the burning of widows); nevertheless Sati, the Incarnation of Dea who immolates Herself in the sacrificial fire, is the type of the Sacrificial Daughter as seen in other cultures under such names as Persephone, Ishtar and Inanna. Thus Sati is a form of the Daughter as Sacrificial Saviour.

We know Thee to be Mahalakshmi, we meditate on Thee as the underlying Power of all things.
O Mother, shed Thy light on us, that we may know Thee through meditation.

Commentary

We know Thee to be Mahalakshmi,

Sri Lakshmi, Great Lakshmi (Maha Lakshmi), is another form of Dea that goes back beyond Vedic times, but unlike Vac and Aditi, She is worshipped by millions under this name today. While attempts have been made to bring Mahalakshmi into the patriarchal ambit, she remains the Great Mother, the Giver of both worldly enjoyment and spiritual realisation.

we meditate on Thee as the underlying Power of all things.

"Underlying Power" is our translation of the word *Shakti*. Those familiar with Hinduism will be aware that in patriarchal usage a Shakti designates the female power of a male god but there is no doubt in the *Devi Gita* that Dea is the One Supreme Deity and Her Shakti is Herself.

O Mother, shed Thy light on us, that we may know Thee through meditation.

This verse is used as a preparation to meditation. It also reminds us of the fundamental spiritual truth that it is only through Her Grace that we may come to Her; only through Her Light that we may see Her; only through Her Love that we may love Her.

O Dea! Obeisance to Thee in the shining order of the world-body; obeisance to Thee in the subtle thread of the world-spirit.
Obeisance to thee in the Unmanifest State; obeisance to thee in the glorious form of Absolute Deity.
O Dea! Obeisance to Thee in the shining order of the world-body;

Commentary

The Cosmos is the body of Dea (*viraj*). The word comes from a root meaning both to rule and to shine. Thus, the Cosmos as the Body of Dea is the Cosmos in thamë, manifesting perfectly the Golden Order.

obeisance to Thee in the subtle thread of the world-spirit.

Through this world-body runs the thread-spirit (*Strivatë*) whereon all the worlds are threaded like pearls upon a string.

Obeisance to thee in the Unmanifest State; obeisance to thee in the glorious form of Absolute Deity.

While Dea is both the body and the soul of the manifest world, she also precedes manifestation. She is not limited by the manifestation of the physical universe or the non-physical universes. Ultimately, She is Absolute Deity (*Brahman*), beyond being and non-being: in Filianic terms, the Dark Mother.

The four half-lines of this verse describe the four cosmic aspects of the Supreme Being, reflected in the human microcosm as the four states: the waking state, dreaming sleep, deep and dreamless sleep and the final state of pure Spiritual Realisation. The *Mandukya Upanishad* relates these states to the three component sounds of OM (or AUM): A-U-M. A is the waking state (or world-body), U is the sleeping state (or world-spirit) M is dreamless sleep (or the Unmanifest Causal Body of Dea) and Absolute Deity is the AUM taken as a whole.

Note that the A is pronounced like the e in "her", U as in "put" and M like the Me in "Merchant".

Through Thy power of nescience doth the world appear, like to a rope appearing as a serpent or as a garland of flowers. Through Thy power of Knowledge Thou dissolvest the world back into thine own Self. Glory unto Thee, the Empress of the Universe.

Commentary

Through Thy power of nescience doth the world appear,

"Nescience" here is an advanced metaphysical concept. It would be usual to translate it simply as "ignorance", but this would inevitably have false connotations for the Western ear. The Sanskrit term is *avidya:* ignorance, or most literally non-(right)-seeing. *Vidya* is closely related to Latin *video,* "I see", and thus to English words such as *vision. A-vidya* is simply *vidya* with the privative *a-* (as in *a*moral or *a*gnostic).

What we need to understand is that, in traditional thought, ignorance is not a mere negative, but is an actual entity—a barrier between ourselves and the innate Knowledge of Truth that we possess. Thus the Tibetan lama makes the *dorje* gesture when teaching an important point. The *dorje* is the thunderbolt that breaks through the barrier of ignorance. In Greek the word for truth is *alethea* "unforgetting" (forgetfulness = *lethe*). Truth is in us, and ignorance is that which prevents us from seeing it.

Ultimately the Truth is that there is nothing other than Dea. So the appearance of the world is, in a sense, an illusion. Or to put it another way, manifestation itself—the Creation—is dependent upon *avidya*. Without *avidya*, nescience, there is no universe.

The path to Pure Enlightenment consists of destroying *avidya* and seeing through the illusion of the world. Thus the simplistic Western mind in the Kali Yuga, having grasped this point, is apt to reason that *avidya* is simply a Bad Thing. But actually it is not that simple. For souls who are not at the stage of Enlightenment, our Mother creates this beautiful world as a haven. And this world-haven is created from her power of nescience or *avidya*. The heaven-worlds, to which Her devotees may attain who have loved Her but not achieved Enlightenment, are likewise manifested through Her power of *avidya*.

like to a rope appearing as a serpent or as a garland of flowers.

The appearance of the world through ignorance, just as a rope in the half-light may appear to be a snake, is a traditional Vedantic image. The image of the garland of flowers, uncommon in patriarchal texts, stresses the beauty and variety of the lovely world created by Dea. Note that these images very literally present the metaphor of *seeing* mistakenly

Through Thy power of Knowledge dost Thou dissolve the world back into Thine own Self.

But ultimately Her opposite power of *vidya*—knowledge or Truth—will dissolve the manifest world back into Herself, whether at the Enlightenment of the individual soul or at the end of time. Thus, in Her aspect as the Dark Mother, the Destroyer of the Worlds, She may seem terrifying to the unenlightened, but She is ultimately the Highest Good.

Glory unto Thee, the Empress of the Universe.

Thus this statement is followed by a *gloria*. To quote from the Daughter Mythos: "She will do what She will do, and blessed is Her Name".

We glorify Her, Who is pure consciousness and whose essence is *That*.

59

Whose being is Bliss unmelded, Whom all the Scriptures know as their final goal.

Commentary

We glorify Her, Who is pure consciousness

It is the consciousness of Dea that upholds the world. She is the one Consciousness of the cosmos, of whom every lesser consciousness (including you, dear reader) is but a fragment.

The word for consciousness here is *Chit*, the middle term of the formula *Sat, Chit, Ananda*—Being, Consciousness and Bliss. In the next line She is also referred to as Bliss, while Dea as Being—both the Being of the universe and the Being that lies beyond it—is the subject of these two verses.

and whose essence is *That*.

The word *That (Tat)* comes from the great Vedantic formulation, **Tat tvam asi:** "That thou art". Here That (*Tat*) means the supreme Brahman, absolute Deity, while *tvam* (thou) is the individual, or fragmentary soul, the *jivatma*. The meaning of the saying is that ultimately the soul is none other than Deity, if only the veil of *avidya* were drawn aside. Realisation, or Enlightenment, is the ultimate understanding that neither the universe nor the individual self is anything other than Dea.

This verse makes it clear that God the Mother is *Tat*—absolute Brahman and thus the Supreme Goal of the Vedas (Scriptures).

Thou transcendest the five bodies. Thou art the Witness of the three states of consciousness.

Thou art the essence of the fragmentary soul, known by the name of *thou*.

Commentary

Thou transcendest the five bodies.

The five bodies, or sheaths (*kosas*), are the vehicles of the soul.

They enclose the fragmentary (individual) soul, or *jiva*, like the successive skins of an onion, each enclosing all those within it, and enclosed by those outside it. A full explication of the kosas would be a study in itself.

Only the first of these five bodies, the "food sheath" (*anna maya kosa*) refers to the physical body. The others are subtler than the level of matter recognised by modern Western science, though still material.

It should be realised that in traditional thought, whatever applies to the human microcosm applies also to the macrocosm of the universe, thus Dea transcends the gross subtle and causal bodies of all things.

Thou art the Witness of the three states of consciousness.

Similarly, as the Witness of the three states of consciousness (waking, dreaming and dreamless sleep), Dea is She who causes these states but is not part of them. She is the essence of the fourth or transcendent state signified by the entirety of the word OM (AUM).

Thou art the essence of the fragmentary soul, known by the name of *thou*.

In the previous verse it is explained that Dea is the *That (tat)* of the Upanishadic **Tat tvam asi** ("That thou art"), in other words, She is the Absolute Brahman or Deity. Now it is made clear that She is also, in essence, the second term: *thou* (*tvam:* root *tv/tu*, common to Latin *tu*, Greek *thu*, German *du*, and English *thou*, from earlier *thu*).

She is both the Atman, the All-Spirit, and the individual fragmentary soul in its essence. In the end there is nothing that is not Dea.

So the Enlightened soul sees Dea in every being. Thus when the Aristasian bows and greets others with the greeting *Rayati* (hail to the Sun in thee), she is acknowledging that each one of us is ultimately not other than Dea.

O Mother! Hail to Thee who art OM, the primordial Word.

**Hail to Thee Who pervadest all as HRIM.
Hail to thee, Mother of all sacred sounds. All-compassionate
Mother, we bow down at Thy lotus feet.**

Commentary

**O Mother! Hail to Thee who art OM, the primordial Word.
Hail to Thee Who pervadest all as HRIM.**

While OM (AUM)represents the primordial Word, HRIM is the
audial embodiment of the World Mother that reverberates
throughout the universe and through the hearts of all beings,
uniting all opposites in the perfect harmony of the Golden Order (*thamë*). Thus the two sacred syllables, each representing the
primordial Unheard Word, represent, respectively, Dea transcendent and Dea immanent in Her creation.

Hail to thee, Mother of all sacred sounds.

From the Primordial Word, all sacred sounds (*mantras*) unfold,
and from the sacred sounds of the Angelic Language proceed
all sounds, all words, all language.

All-compassionate Mother, we bow down at Thy lotus feet.

Our Mother has compassion on the whole world and we, like
the Angels, bow down at Her lotus feet. Wherever we see Sri
Lakshmi standing, Her feet rest on a blossoming lotus: for it is
where Her feet touch the waters of substance that the universe
blossoms forth.

The Lotus feet of Dea create for us the beautiful earth and
the heavens, wherein we may live and find refuge. They also
create the vision of our Mother, wherein we may find both
worldly enjoyment and eternal bliss.

All hail the World-Mother! Take refuge at Her lotus feet!

Isa Upanishad

Feminine Translation

ALL THIS is whole; and That is whole also. This wholeness has come from That wholeness. And when this wholeness is merged in That wholeness, all that remains is wholeness.

AUM
Shantih, shantih, shantih

1. All that turns in this turning world is indwelt by Dea. By renouncing the unreal, guard your True Self. And covet you not the wealth of any maiden.

2. She who would live a hundred years in this world; let her work the works of thamë. For only when the werdës are in thamë may they not cleave to a maiden.

3. The worlds of the demons are wrapped in unseeing darkness; to these worlds, after death, go those maidens that slay the True Self.

4. Unmoving, yet swifter than mind, beyond reach of the senses, the True Self moves before them forever, yet stays ever still. Than the swiftest of all those that run is the True Self yet swifter. In the Wind that is soul of the world, she ordains every work.

5. For She moves and is still, She is far, She is near, She is outside of all, yet within all.

6. The wise maid sees all beings in her true Self and her True Self within all beings. How can she then have hate for any?

7. To she who sees, all beings become one within her own True Self. What delusion can bind, what sorrow can touch, the maid who sees the Oneness of all?

8. For She pervades all. She is radiant, yet bodiless; without muscle, without injury, pure and unsullied by evil. She is the Seer and She is the Thinker; indwelling in all, and Self-existent. She has ordained all in thamë for eternal years.

9. Into great darkness falls she who worships merely nescience. Into greater darkness yet falls she who worships knowledge.

10. Distinct they say is the fruit of knowledge, and distinct the fruit of nescience. So say the learned Elder Mothers to whom the world owes its wisdom.

11. She who knows both knowledge and nescience crosses death through nescience and gains immortality through knowledge.

12. Into great darkness falls she who worships the merely manifest. Into greater darkness yet falls she who worships the unmanifest.

13. Distinct they say is the fruit of the worship of the manifest, and distinct the fruit of the unmanifest. So say the learned Elder Mothers to whom the world owes its wisdom.

14. She who knows both the manifest and the unmanifest crosses death through the unmanifest and gains immortality through the manifest.

15. The face of Truth is covered with a golden disc. O Radiant Mistress, uncover that we who adore Truth may behold.

16. O Radiant Mistress, sole Traveller of the heavens, O Lady Sun, Daughter of the Golden Womb, withdraw Thy rays and ingather Thy burning effulgence. Now would I see, by Thy Grace, Thy fair Form, the pure Essence of all. For I know that That also am I.

17. Now may my life-breath return to the One Breath and may my body be burned to ashes. AUM. O mind, remember what has been done. Intelligence remember. Remember, O remember.

18. O Annya, great Fire. O Dea, knower of all our deeds; lead us along the good path, whereby we may enjoy in purity the fruits of our action. Destroy our deceitful sins. Reverence, prostration and words of prayer we bring Thee again and again.

A note on this translation of the Isa Upanishad

The translation of the Upanishads into standard modern English is near-impossible, since the translation is from Sanskrit—a language which is both replete with metaphysical terminology and retains many of the metaphysical "root-implications" of more "ordinary" words. English, on the other hand, has been refined over centuries into one of the most "practical" and "down-to-earth" languages even among the Western tongues; and while it has a fine vocabulary for physical and even emotional beauty, it is less well equipped to deal with metaphysics (especially poetic and non-technical metaphysics) than almost any other. However, what we say of English is scarcely less applicable to any Western language.

Translators are necessarily driven to the use of technical terms, special *ad-hoc* coinages, untranslated Sanskrit words or awkward circumlocutions.

As Filianic Déanists, we have access to a terminology that can far more accurately render the concepts of Sanskrit Scripture. Words like *thamë, werdë, raya* etc, which have no equivalent in English, but are very close in meaning to the equivalent Sanskrit terms; and concepts like that of the True Self, which is fundamental to Filianic thealogy, are in everyday use among Aristasians and other Déanists. They allow Sanskrit Scripture to be rendered in terms that are familiar and neither awkward nor inaccurate, so that they may be read as they were intended to be read.

The Sanskrit Scriptures may still be "difficult" (many of them treat of a High Mysticism which is by its nature hard for the worldly soul to grasp) but the artificial barrier of language may at least be largely eliminated.

This is not an answer to the general "problem of translation", since Déanic vocabulary is as obscure to the average English person as the original Sanskrit.

But these translations are made specifically for devotees of Our Mother God. Their sole intention is to be valuable to such devotees. And, since we are exiled in a world where we have no living tradition, perhaps there is a special Providence in the fact that they *can* be valuable to us as they can to few other Western people.

Commentary

All that turns in this turning world: All that belongs to the sublunary world of flux and change. Literally, all that belongs to the world of *werdë* which means both fate and worldly activity and literally *turning* as well as *becoming* (as opposed to pure Being).

guard your True Self: The True Self is an important concept in Déanic Moral Thealogy. The concepts of the True and false selves accord with the traditional doctrine that "there are two in us". In everyday use, the True Self is often used to mean simply one's "better self"—the self that belongs wholly to Dea—and since the concept can be applied at many levels, this is perfectly accurate. However, in the fullest sense, the True Self is beyond one's own individual personality. She is the Indwelling Spirit Herself, the Atma (a word that in Sanskrit means both Breath/Spirit and "self" in both the higher and the everyday sense).

When Our Lady says, "For the Spirit is One, and I am the Spirit; and you are the Spirit also in the innermost temple of your heart",(*The Temple of the Heart*, V. 12) it is to this one True Self or Spirit that She is referring.

For only when the werdës are in thamë may they not cleave to a maiden: We are dealing here with the doctrine of *karma yoga*, which is a fundamental theme of Isa Upanishad—the concept of salvation by "work". Work (*karma*) in this sense seems ambiguous for the West Tellurian mind, because it can mean both everyday activity and ritual action. For traditional people, the distinction between the two things is much less absolute.

In Déanic language, the concepts of werdë and thamë are often joined (Sai Werdë is said to be the daughter of Sai Thamë). What is being said here is that when werdë (in the sense of action, work, worldly activity) is in thamë (meaning ritualised and in harmony with the Golden Order), only then does it not cling to a maid (in the sense of the popular Western usage of "karma", which is legitimate but partial) and become what Déanists term "a werdë": that is, an "accretion" that affects us for good or ill from one birth to another.

the Wind that is soul of the world: Sai Vaya, the Wind-Spirit—Who is, of course not truly other than the Spirit in Her other "Forms".

So say the learned Elder Mothers to whom the world owes its wisdom: The learned Elder Mothers are our honoured Ancestresses who transmitted primordial Truth from generation to generation from the beginning. Since the text here is affirming the continuity of Isa Upanishad with the Primordial Tradition, the un-patriarchalised form is clearly more accurate.

Into great darkness falls she who worships merely nescience. Into greater darkness yet falls she who worships knowledge: This and the parallel statement about the manifest and the unmanifest have been subject to various interpretations. What we should understand is that nescience, in Déanic usage, is the precise equivalent to the Sanskrit *avidya*: non-knowledge, or ignorance in a very special sense. Since the world is ultimately illusion, it is only through nescience that it exists. Pure Knowledge in the highest sense will dispel it.

However, while this seems like a straightforward "anti-worldly" perspective, the force of nescience as a creative power is actually seen positively in many contexts—especially where Dea is being worshipped in Her original feminine form.

Thus in the Angelic Hymn from the *Devi Gita* we read:

Through Thy power of nescience doth the world appear, like to a rope appearing as a serpent or as a garland of flowers.
Through Thy power of Knowledge Thou dissolvest the world back into thine own Self. Glory unto Thee, O Empress of the Universe.

We must therefore remember—whatever other interpretations may be applied to the Isa Upanishad—that it has to do with the balance between the world-creating nescience and the world-transcending knowledge, just as much of the Isa Upanishad deals with the legitimate fruits of action (werdë which is in thamë) as opposed to pure renunciation, in accordance with the words of the Great Hymn to Mahalakshmi from the *Padma Purana*:

> *O Dea, Mahalakshmi,*
> *Thou Art the Giver of Intelligence and success*
> *And of both worldly enjoyment and Liberation*

O Radiant Mistress, sole Traveller of the heavens: here Dea is addressed in Her Form as Sai Raya, the Janya of the Sun. She is also enjoined to withdraw Her brightness that is "too great for maid to look upon", as described in The Creation. Thus, in Filianic terms, Her Daughter-function is being appealed to.

Thy fair Form, the pure Essence of all: "Essence of all" translates Sanskrit *purusha* which in Aristasian metaphysical terminology is Essence as opposed to substance (*prakriti*). See "The Key to Metaphysics" in *The Feminine Universe*. In some interpretations "the unmanifest" of verses 12. and 13. is considered to be *prakriti* or substance (i.e. that which is "below" manifestation: *sub-stance* is literally that which "stands below"). Essence is also unmanifest, but is that which stands "above" manifestation and may also be seen as the Divine Creative Intelligence. Essence creates the *forms* of all things, which are embedded in, but do not ultimately belong to, "matter".

However, there are other interpretations of "the manifest" and "the unmanifest"—such as the Personal and Impersonal, or Formal and Supra-Formal, aspects of Dea. In Filianic Faith these are represented by the Mother and the Dark Mother (see, e, g, the Filianic Creed).

O Annya, great Fire: Sai Annya the Janya of Fire. As is usual in Isa Upanishad, the Janyati are seen from the highest perspective, as aspects of Dea Herself.

Part III

THE FILIANIC SUTRAS

THE FOLLOWING texts are associated with the Filianic faith although by no means all are explicitly Filianic in doctrine. Like the Mythic texts in the first part of this book, they appear, in these precise forms, to be around thirty years old.

They have been made available in a few slightly differing texts. These, to the best of our knowledge, are the purest versions.

These texts form the only substantial body of Scripture currently available that is wholly feminine and non-patriarchal, while being also wholly orthodox and traditional: untouched by the "New Age" movement, modern Western ideologies and modern Western human-centred (rather than Dea-centred) thought in general.

They have provided an important inspirational and devotional resource for generations of Déanists and Filianists who have sought a pure faith free alike from patriarchal influence and from modernist error.

Aristasians have embraced them as the closest possible equivalent to the faith of an all-feminine world in the equivalent of its Kali Yuga, and indeed their origin in these forms is probably Aristasian.

The term *sutra* has long been used for these texts, although the term used in the names of some of them is *clew*—a word with precisely the same root-meaning as sutra (cf. *suture*): that is "thread". The term refers to the Thread Spirit (*Strivatë*) in Her rôle as Guide and Teacher. The closely-related English word *clue* originates in a direct reference to Ariadne's thread which leads the soul through the labyrinth in Cretan mythology.

The Strivatë is She Who threads all worlds and beings "as pearls upon a string". Her symbolism is the essence of the Rosary. Through the clews, or sutras, the Strivatë threads our souls, binding them back (the literal meaning of *re-ligion*, which is a re-ligaturing) to Our Mother God.

The Heart of Water

Authorised Version

PLACE WHOLLY thy trust in the Spirit, My Mother, for She is the Rich, the all-sufficient.

2. What canst thou lack if thou art Hers? For the whole of creation is thine.

3. Walk gently on the earth, for the earth is thy sister, and the creatures thereof are thy kin.

4. I have set maids to watch upon them; treat them not, then, with hardness.

5. Raise not thy voice above the gentle tone except it be in song, nor seek to place thyself above another, for the spirit in each is a ray of the Spirit My Mother, and as thou render service unto them, so servest thou also Her.

6. Walk thou in meekness on the earth, forgive all ills, and treat all souls as thou wouldst thyself be treated.

7. The hard shall break, the mighty shall fail, but the supple shall endure for ever.

8. There is no thing strong but shall meet a stronger, yet where is the hand that shall break water?

9. The hard find not the Spirit My Mother, for their hearts are frozen, like to the hard and brittle ice.

10. In their own might they suppose themselves to stand, yet how mighty is the tree whose roots are not in the deep earth?

11. And the roaring river, how long shall she flow when she is severed from the source?

12. The icy heart shall break, for it rests upon illusion, yet the heart of water shall endure.

13. The heart of water is not proud, she trusts not in herself. She seeks not power nor authority of herself, for there is no authority save in the Spirit My Mother.

14. I am every priestess and every mother, each princess and each lady of the earth, and none has authority save in Me. Therefore obey me in thy lady, for I am thy Lady in her.

15. The heart of water is all obedience, nor hardens against her lady. The heart of water lays claim to nothing, therefore possesses all things.

16. Authority flows from the heart of water because she possesses none. The heart of ice has not authority, neither flows it from her.

17. Authority in the name of maids is false, and the disobedient may not command. When the heart of ice seizes the reins there is strife and contention, for each icy heart seeks to possess the world.

18. Where authority is not, there is no agreement, where hardness prevails, the waters cannot flow.

19. When each spoke assays to be the centre, the wheel cannot turn.

20. Who rules in her own right is a tyrant, or yet in the right of other maids. There is but one authority and the Truth alone is true.

21. Eat not the bread of tyrants nor drink their drink, but offer them first to She that owns them.

22. Join not their contentions, neither be a party to one side nor to the other, for they are athamë.

23. Thou shalt obey thy Lady, though all the world deny Her; and thus obey each lady of the earth whose authority flows from the fountainhead of Her Truth,

24. Yea, though the world pay them not honour and power lie in the hand of tyranny.

25. For though in this place thou seemest but a few, and Her servants reduced to a remnant, yet in truth the age of the unbelievers is but a moment in the endless stream of time;

26. And this world but a grain of sand on the shore of unnumbered worlds.

27. In truth thou art surrounded by the bright host of Her children, serried through time and space, in whose light the unbelievers are but the remnant of a remnant, and their world but a cobweb in the midst of a glittering palace.

28. And thou art one with that shining host; each radiant soul is thy sister.

29. Who lives in true obedience is free, for Her service is perfect freedom;

30. But the disobedient are slaves; puppets of the passions and the senses, with no true will.

31. Those who do evil are the slaves of evil, their freedom is but an illusion.

32. Let the maid obey the mistress, let the mistress obey the countess, let the countess obey the duchess, let the duchess obey the rayin.

33. Let the rayin obey the empress, let the empress give obedience unto Me.

34. Let the younger sister obey the elder, let the child obey the mother, let the mother obey the priestess, let the priestess give obedience unto Me. Let the pupil obey the ranya, let the scholar obey the rani. Thus shall all things be in harmony and harmony be in all things.

35. Fear not the way of obedience, for in that way art thou wholly secure. Let thy Mistress direct thee and thou shalt be led unto the perfect garden of Avala.

36. To rest in the hands of a mistress that ruleth in thamë is to rest in Mine own hands, and I shall enfold thee in the hand of love and keep thee in a gentle safe-keeping.

37. But she that followeth not the path of obedience resteth in the hands of the passions, whose wild winds blow this way and that;

38. She giveth obedience to the demons of the wind that lead her not into safety, but toss her upon the storm. They raise her up only to throw her down and take delight in her anguish.

39. The way of obedience is a safe harbour and a well-made vessel that shall bear the soul unto the nether shore.

40. A golden chain of love doth link each maid with her mistress,

41. From the humblest of them that love Me unto the very Janyati of Heaven;

42. A golden chain from the summit of the mountain unto the deepest depth.

43. And it shall lift up each soul to the golden land of Avala, and to the yet more beauteous lands beyond.

44. If a maiden rule by authority of thamë and yet obeyeth not; if thamë is broken her heart is turned to ice;

45. Let her be made the least among the children and be the servant of those she has wrongly ruled.

46. Let her feel the chastening willow-rod and feel also the love of her mistress until her heart be melted.

47. But them that rule not by authority of thamë, whose dominion floweth not from the love of My Mother;

48. Truly the gates of their empire shall be shattered, even as the gates of Hell.

49. They that live in discord with eternal harmony; in discord shall they perish.

50. Their cities that stand so proud upon the morning shall be rended asunder before the even come. No pillar shall stand erect, nor any stone lie whole upon another.

51. The empire that has not thamë its foundation; that resteth upon the world for its support; that beareth false truth emblaz'd upon its banner; is like to a city builded on the ice.

52. The tyrant that the dark queen doth make her puppet, to rule in falsehood and to strangle truth; like to a mirror broken and perverted, reflecting true thamë rent from its true form;

53. Into what darkness shall her actions lead her? Truly, her actions forge an iron chain to bind her fast and suffer no release.

54. That these dark latter times should come upon thee, was it not known before the dawn of time?

55. That the heart of ice should rule the heart of water and ignorance seize the reins in every land.

56. That the wicked should ride aloft in a golden chariot and the wise and the good be trampled to the earth.

57. Evil must needs arise and be triumphant, and the dark mistress have her night of power.

58. Yet dark is the path of them that prepare her entry, and swiftly shall they behold the night of blood;

59. For she is the dragon that doth devour her children and casteth her servants into the lake of fire.

60. And whatso shall pass within the earthly empire shall pass within the empire of the soul.

61. Follow thou, then, the gentle way of thamë; let not thy heart be taken by the ice.

62. Let her sweet waters flow unto thy Mother, tread thou the way of quietness and love.

63. Follow this way and thou shalt see perfection. The sun shall rise and scatter the darkness hence.

64And after the long and wearisome night-journey, thou shalt behold the light of the golden dawn.

The Mantle

Authorised Version

YOU that are weary of the world, you that are lonely; you that have suffered hardship, that have suffered hurt: come, gather about Me and be you enfolded in My mantle.

2. In the inner silence you shall hear Me, and in the inner darkness shall you see Me.

3. And the future shall be better than the past.

4. Come, seek protection beneath My mantle, for I have turned no creature from Me, be you sheltered in the folds of My garment.

5. For the ills of the world shall pass away, even as the terrors of the night.

6. And the dawn shall be bright with splendour and sweet with the singing of the blessed souls.

7. And I shall be your comfort in the darkness.

The Clew Of The Horse

Authorised Version

EARTH MOVES, but Heaven is still. The rim revolves, but the Centre remains without motion.

2. Yet from the still point all movement comes; and Earth is the shadow of Heaven. 3. Space doth extend without limit, nor is there any boundary to the worlds, but the Point is without extension; yet from the Point alone all space proceedeth. 4. All manifest things are bound to the three times; of that which is, which was, which is to come; but the Moment is without time. It neither is nor was, nor ever will be.

5. Yet the Moment is seed and germ of time; the timeless spring wherein time's mighty river hath its rise.

6. The Point and the Moment and the timeless Centre; these three are One and the One is the Spirit. 7. Each manifest thing hath a cause, and each cause hath a cause before it, but the First Cause hath no cause before Her, for She is the Spirit.

8. She that acts not is the Cause of all action. She that is not is the Cause of all being. She that is still is the Centre and Source of all movement.

9. At the rim is the movement greatest; close unto the centre is it least. 10. Where there is no movement there is purity. 11. The Spirit in maid loveth purity, yet her mind doth distract her. The mind craveth peace, yet it is made mad by the poisons. 12. The poisons are three, and the first of the three is named folly. 13. Folly is that forgetfulness that doth stand between maid and the truth, like to an hoodwink that darkens her eyes. 14. And even when her mind doth seize the truth is her stomach beglamoured by the veil of illusion. 15. Desire and hatred are the other twain; that which pursues and grasps the way of pleasure; that which avoids and shuns the way of pain. 16. These two must keep the wheel forever turning; the two blind

oxen that drive it ever round.

17. Yet what can come of this but pain and sorrow? Whatever moves can never come to rest. 18. All things, once gained, must pass into the darkness; all things, once built, must crumble into dust.

19. Sickness, old age and death must come to all maids; what thing within this life should'st thou pursue? 20. Thy fairest hopes undone bring desolation, or else, fulfilled, shall vanish in a day. 21. Life is a passing dream; of all its treasures, there is no thing among them shall endure.

22. Restrain thy soul from chasing bright illusions. Let her return to purity again. 23. Thus shall she come once more to the still Centre, thus shall she stay upon her Mother's breast. 24. Chasten thy soul with shame and make her humble; thus shall she come to peace and sweet repose. 25. When she has ceased from all movement, then she and the Centre are one.

26. In the lucid darkness, in the indrawn breath, from whence all comes, whereto all must return, there lie two: the one and the many. 27. The first is called by the name of wisdom, the second by the name of folly. 28. And still beyond these two is She that doth govern them both, like to a maid that breathes both in and out.

29. She rules both the rivers and the wellsprings, the wellsprings and the mighty sea. 30. When the Word was spoken and the worlds were born, She did observe in silence. 31. Her webs She did outweave; both longwise and crosswise did She spread them, to cover every corner of the field. 32. These will She draw together when that their time is come. 33. All the holy Ranyas are Her servants; the craftmaids are created by Her craft. Doth govern all, and all She will ingather when the worlds are rolled up like to a parchment scroll.

34. And even as the splendid sun, singing aloud in her brightness, doth shine unto the heights and to the depths, and all the four directions, so doth She govern all that hath come to birth.

35. She that doth unfold all things like to a rose from the seed of Her being; She that doth nurture unto fullness each thing that hath fullness within it; She that doth scatter the colours, 'tis She that doth govern the world.

36. But She that taketh the colours upon Her, that doth work the soil and also eat the grain; She doth partake of the fruits of Her working. 37. All shapes She doth assume, and every form and likeness; for She is of three strains commingled. 38. Three paths She doth follow, and Her road doth wind according to Her works.

39. Like to the size of a maiden's thumb She is, and radiant as the sun, when thought and will have harbour in Her bosom. 40. But when knowing and being are all of Her workings, then She is like to another, no greater than the point of a needle.

41. Think that She is but a part of the hundredth part of an hair's tip, divided an hundred times. Yet She is like to all the manifest world. 42. No form She hath, nor colour, no scent nor any savour; yet all things that She doth enter, She becometh.

43. According to the acts that She performeth, and the choices wherewith they are directed; 44. By these She doth take on unnumbered shapes, and numberless conditions doth She enter.

45. She that hath no beginning nor any end; She that did stand in the heart of chaos and make all things harmonious, She that doth bear the worlds within Her hand; the maid that knoweth Her is truly free.

46. She that is the maker of being and of unbeing; She that is all that is and all that is not; the maid that knoweth her in truth hath left all worlds; hath left in truth the body and the mind.

47. Thou art not thy body, nor is thy body any portion of thee. 48. It is an estate which thou hold'st for a time, and after a time shall pass from thee. 49. Therefore, have thou governance of thy body, nor let it be in any thing thy ruler. 50. Keep it in purity as a temple built of earth and a place of devotion.

51. Thou art not thy mind, nor is thy mind any portion of thee. 52. It is an estate which thou hold'st for a time, and after a time shall pass from thee. 53. For longer than the body shalt thou hold it; and when the body passeth into dust, still it shall be with thee. 54. Yet in its turn shall it pass away, and in its appointed season. 55. But thou shalt never pass away; when all the worlds are dust thou shalt endure.

56. Therefore, have thou governance of thy mind, nor let it be in any thing thy ruler. 57. Keep it in purity as a temple built of air and a place of devotion.

58. Hard to govern is the mind, like to a proud horse that drinketh the wind, filled with its own desires. 59. Fain would it draw the rein from thy hand and carry you where it will; fain would it take the body for its mistress. 60. Like to a bird that doth hop from twig to twig, turning first to one fruit, then to another, without control or constancy.

61. Yet calm the mind and bring it to the garden of thy Lady; to the peaceful garden to rest by gentle streams. 62. By long training is it brought to contemplation; is it bridled that it may tread the heavens.

63. Let it be in harmony in all things. In the smallest actions, let its steps be measured. 64. Let the body obey her in her harmony, that all works show forth control, respect and courtesy. 65. As in a dance, the two shall act together, as in a dance where each doth know her part. 66. For if thy horse run loose upon the high-road, how shalt thou learn to ride among the stars?

The Sermon of the Apple-Seed

Authorised Version

FROM THE branch of a tree Our Lady plucked an apple, and She split the apple in two halves, so that the five-pointed star formed by its seeds might be seen. 2. And She removed the seed representing the topmost point, and held it in the palm of Her hand. And She spoke, saying:

3. Like to this apple-seed is all the teaching I have given and shall give to you. 4. Like to the full apple is all the knowledge relative to your sphere of being. 5. Like to all the other apples of the tree is the knowledge relative to all the numberless spheres.

6. But behind these spheres lies a deeper reality; changeless, beyond the impermanent flux of time. 7. For even as the apple turns from bud to bloom, from blossom to the fruit; ripens, matures, decays and is reborn; 8. So also shall the spheres and galaxies, the subtle realms, the sure and solid earth; so shall all these in their season pass away, and in their season be reborn again. 9. Thus has it been ten thousand times before, and countless times again, thus shall it be.

10. But knowledge of the Truth beyond this flux is like to knowledge of the tree itself, which changes not while the fruit is born and dies. 11. Like to the spreading boughs is the Love that sustains all creation which is fallen from pure Spirit. 12. Like to the bole is that Spirit Herself, from whom all creation flows. 13. And still beneath the branches and the bole lie the roots in darkness, like unto She that is beyond both being and unbeing; 14. And even as the tree's roots are not seen, so can there be no knowledge of the Absolute; for to know Her is to have passed beyond knowing.

15. And from this tree of all knowledge and of the boundaries beyond which knowledge can not pass, I have given to you but the seed of one apple.

16. For I am come that you may have deliverance. 17. There are many questions concerning the nature of things and of being whose answers you may know, or partly know; and many whose answers lie beyond the understanding possible to you.

18. But I am not sent to discourse with you upon these matters, but to lead you to deliverance in perfection. 19. And all the knowledge that shall bring you to deliverance is contained within the seed of an apple.

20. Yet within the seed is the essence of the tree, and from the seed the whole tree may unfold. 21. So from essential Truth unfolds all other knowledge, even as the music of the spheres unfolds from a single note.

22. Therefore when you think upon the questions of life, of time, of seasons or the spheres, contemplate first the seed of Truth, and let your thoughts unfold from that seed. 23. Let the pure and single note of Truth attune your soul. Then shall mind rise up into soul, and soul breathe the breath of Spirit.

24. This do, and your thoughts shall be harmonic with the universal music of Eternity. 25. But let your thoughts grow from lower or from lesser or from merely accidental things, and they shall wax rank and dissonant; 26. For it cannot be that the Tree of Life shall grow from the seed of a nettle.

27. If her thoughts are bound to accidental things, the soul cannot attain to liberation.

28. Dissonant and jarring with eternal Harmony, the little sphere is severed from the great.

29. Seek not for certainty in any thing beyond the seed of Truth. 30. That the sky is above you and the earth below; that you breathe and eat and move - to these and to many things must you give your assent that the life of the world may proceed. 31. Yet even of these there is no certainty, for the world is but a dream from which you must some day awaken.

32. Within the world you may be certain only of that Truth which my Mother has given from beyond the world. 33. There-

fore know you well the sacred Mythos and the words that I reveal to you, 34. And let your knowledge dwell not only on the surface, but go deep into the inner soul; and let this knowledge be the seed of all your knowing. 35. For the holy Word cries not in the market-place, but whispers in the heart of every soul that Truth which she alone may understand.

36. It is not needful that you should seek knowledge of the highest things outside the sacred Mythos and My words. 37. For I have revealed to you all that is needful that you should attain liberation; and what I have not revealed, that is not needful.

38. But if you shall discourse on that which is not needful, I give to you three words. Let you not become forgetful of them: 39. That there can be no certainty beyond the seed of Truth, therefore you may speak of likelihood only; 40. That you shall let your speculation be harmonic with the seed of Truth, for speculation that is dissonant gives not knowledge, but leads to the abyss of those that have rejected Truth; 41. And you that have care of My children, let them not become confounded by dissonant thought and work.

42. But beyond all else is this word: that the purpose of speculation is that mind and soul shall grow with the seed of Truth, 43. And any discourse that leads away from inward love of Truth; be that discourse high and pure, be it even harmonic, yet it is the spawn of khear, and you, My children, shall turn from it.

44. Yet be not afraid, for the seed of Truth shall be your guide and your protector and shall bring you to deliverance. 45. And I give to you one word which shall conquer every danger. 46. That word is love, and the humility that flows from love. 47. Receive with love the seed of Truth and all things shall be well.

Thoughts of the Mind

Authorised Version

THOUGHTS of the mind pass not away, nor vanish into air.

2. For every thought is a builder in the subtle world that lies about you.

3. Thoughts of beauty and of things of the Spirit refine and purify the soul, making her fair to look upon and graceful in her movements,

4. Uniting her with the universal music of eternity and gathering about her the servants of the Janyati.

5. But harsh thoughts harden the soul; coarse thoughts coarsen the soul; thoughts bound only to the things of clay burden the soul with heavy chains.

6. My children, I speak not in pictures, for truly these things are; and to be seen by all whose eyes may pierce the veil of illusion.

7. What maiden, receiving of her mother a fine and well-made house of well-wrought oak and stone and furnished by the skilful hand of love, will break the walls and furnishings, pour filthy waters into every place and bring swine to dwell in the most splendid chambers?

8. Will she not rather bring new things of beauty and precious works of love to add to those that lie already there?

9. Will she not keep away all dirt and defilement and protect it from all harm?

11. Knows she not that the thoughts of her mind pass not away, nor vanish into air?

12. Knows she not that every thought of greed, of hate, of lust, of anger is a scar upon her subtle body?

13. Sees she not that she surrounds herself with hateful things that are the forms of her thoughts?

14. Sees she not that evil demons harbour in these forms even as rats infest a dunghill?

15. And does she not know that when her mortal body is

passed into the earth she will have no place wherein to dwell save in that subtle body her thoughts have so misshaped, and among the forms of her creation?

16. Let the soul rather fill her dwelling with the warmth of love and generosity, with the sweet, cool air of purity, with the flowers of simplicity, humility and gentleness.

17. Let her garden flow with the fountains of virtue and lie open to the sunlight of our Mother's love.

18. Let the soul lie only open and the sunlight will stream in, filling her with joy and warmth and beauty; for truly your Mother loves you and delights in giving Her grace.

19. Then be not bound by the world of clay, but turn your thoughts upon Eternity, and the path of light shall be made clear.

20. Forget not the power of words, for a word has all the power of a thought and a thought has power to move the earth and the heavens.

21. Therefore speak not evil in idleness, nor fall into the custom of ill speaking; but govern your words even as your actions.

22. Speak words of love and innocence, of mildness and of hope, and you shall weave a raiment of peace about your soul, and a veil of gentle light.

23. Speak often prayers; speak them in the rhythm of your steps, attune them to the beating of your heart.

24. For She that governs the endless ages governs also the hour of every action. Let your voice call on Her in pure simplicity, for She is the Lady of the noontide and the Lady of the night, the Lady of the mountain and the valley.

25. Truly, the world is a field of conflict between the powers of good and the legions of the Dark One. In the cycles of civilisations is the conflict manifest, and in the soul of every maid.

26. For the servants of the Dark One fasten upon the false self like to the bindweed upon a growing plant. And the radiant Janyati of heaven stand ready to defend the soul when she shall cry upon them.

27. Truly, there is nothing in the world of clay that happens of itself, for the veil of matter is shot through with the light of the Real and the darkness of the false.

28. And not a sparrow lights upon a twig but it shows forth the conflict between evil and the Good, nor any grain of sand shifts in the desert reflecting not some spiritual truth;

29. neither does a star fall in the farthest corner of the firmament without an inward meaning.

30. What then is the wisdom of this world, that knows the outward shows of things but not their inward truth?

31. The wisdom of the world is good for the world, but what when the world shall pass away?

32. If the navigator can no longer use her legs, how shall she fare when her vessel is cast up upon the shore?

33. Look without and you shall see within; look within and you shall see without.

34. For I am the inwardness of all things:

35. I am between the ripple and the water; I am between the music and the song; I am between the breathing and the breath; between the lightest word of greeting and the thought from which it flows.

36. You have stripped away layer after layer of the world to seek what lies within, and have found nothing at the centre; but I was between each layer and every other.

37. Break in two an apple seed and seek to find the tree that shall grow from it. You shall find nothing. Yet the essence of the tree is in the seed.

Even so am I in all things.

The Pillar of Light

Authorised Version

UPON THE HEAVEN are these words inscribed, the words of thy salvation. Upon the Heaven in signs of fire before the dawn of time. Upon the Crystal Tablet that passeth not away.

2. In the tongue of tongues are they inscribed, and in the tongue of Angels that was before all tongues. 3. What is your language of the earth, My children? What are the words of thy speech?

4. Are they not fallen from the first, the mother language? Are they not broken and impaired?

5. Yet I have brought to you a clear recital; a faultless sound of the celestial voice. 6. I have forged your words into a crystal mirror that they may reflect the Truth; and the words that are writ upon the Heaven are transcribed without fault upon the earth.

7. Gaze deep into the crystal mirror and thy heart shall be transformed; hearken to the clear recital. 8. For there is no other Truth than this, nor any way unto salvation.

9. Them that have seen these signs and do not heed them; ignorant they, and full of folly.

10. Hard are their hearts, like to ice that resisteth love's fire. 11. In the things of the world have they rested their trust; they seek Truth in the veil of illusion. 12. An hundred pursuits they pursue, and in them seek contentment.

13. Ask them: where shalt thou hide when the storm is upon thee, and wherein take shelter?

14. An hundred safe places there are and an hundred good havens; even so shall they answer. 15. An hundred most truly there are, yet but one is the Truth, and the ninety and nine are illusion. For this world shall dissolve and its splendours be vanished; its pain and its sorrows shall pass like the summer rain. 16. Life is not long, death is swift in the coming; and the ninety and nine thousand things shall be gone, but the Truth shall remain.

17. The world is but a shadow, yet it is a shadow of Truth; and at the ending of the age shall the world be redeemed. 18. Neither a leaf upon a bramble shall be lost, nor a blade of grass pass into nothingness. 19. But thou, My child, of all the world, thou alone hast power to choose; and thus art thou called maid, for maid is she that hath the power of choosing.

20. Fix then your will upon the Truth and your heart on the Spirit My Mother, for by your love shall the world be redeemed, even to the last blade of grass.

21. In thy work praise Her and in thy resting, in thy speech and in thy silence. 22. For thou wert made one with Her, and this is thy true estate. It is good for a maid to till the soil, but it is better to live with her Lady. It is good to build and to weave, but it is better to live with her Lady. It is good to serve maids in every way, but it is better to live with her Lady.

23. She that liveth wholly with her Lady is the servant of all the world; no labour is so great as this, nor so greatly to be honoured.

24. She that has followed Me upon the mountain liveth wholly with her Lady and treadeth no step without Her. 25. She doth eat not to herself, but to her Lady; she moveth not nor drinketh to herself. 26. Hard is the path upon the mountain and narrow the way. Yet none know joy to its fullest measure save only them that tread it.

27. None shall call upon Me and be lost. Every cry of the world shall I heed; and when the whole of a heart cries upon Me, that soul shall I take beneath My mantle. 28. Cry and thou shalt have answer; love and thou art beloved, hope and thy hope shall be fulfilled, in this world and in all the worlds to come.

29. Hold thou fast to the Truth, for the Truth is a pillar; a steadifast pillar that all the world cannot shake. 30. Not by the breadth of an hair has it moved since time's dawning, neither yet by the breadth of an hair until time have its end. 31. From the uttermost height of the Heaven descendeth the pillar; descendeth it down as a glorious pillar of Light. To the nethermost depths of the hells it descendeth; nor the might of the demons can move it the breadth of an hair.

32. Like to a mist is this world that surroundeth the pillar; to a mist that is swiftly dispelled by the cold wind of death. 33. Hold you fast to the Truth, for the Truth is thy shelter; sure refuge 'gainst which neither death nor the storm shall prevail. 34. This world shall be scattered like straw, and an hundred shall follow; and each in its turn shall be scattered like chaff on the wind. 35. The empires are born and decay, the stars live and perish, but the pillar of Truth moveth not by the breadth of an hair.

36. Like to a play is thy life, and the acting of mummers; like to a painted scene all the things of the world 37. The things of thy life and its acts and its purposes; where shall they be in an hundred score years from this day? Yet an hundred score years are no more than a breath in the measureless life of thy soul.

38. The things thou doest of themselves are nothing; the things thou buildest or that thou destroy; the things the foolish take for life's high purpose are but painted scenes 'gainst which the play is played.

39. For the play is not on earth but in the Heaven, not in the body, nor yet in the mind, but deep within the heart.

40. Truly, the truth of the play is the dance of the soul; 41. her journey through forests and plains, over seas, over mountains; her restless and wearisome quest through the whole of the world; 42. And each step brings her nearer to That which she yearns for in secret; or else, in her ignorance, carries her further away. 43. Like a leaf on the wind is the foolish soul blown without purpose; the plaything of passions, the puppet of every desire; 44. Knowing not whence she comes, nor yet where she is going; seeking substance in shadows and having no heed for the Truth.

45. All the glories of earth are but shadows of Heavenly splendour; all earthly desires but reflections of Heavenly love. 46. Hold you fast to the Truth, for the Truth is thy guide through the labyrinth. Hold you fast to the Truth and thy steps shall be led not astray. 47. Hold you fast to the Truth, and give heed to the lucid recital, for the pillar of Truth moveth not by the breadth of an hair.

The Temple of the Heart

Authorised Version

KNOW YOUR OWN HEART and make examination thereof; for if you know not your own heart, there can be no true knowledge of anything. 2. But within the innermost temple of your heart shall you find the seas and the heavens and all the illimitable cosmos; 3. For the space within this temple is as vast as the manifest universe.

4. The ignorant eye shall not see this temple from without, 5. For it is smaller than the seed of an apple; and smaller than the seventh part of the seed of an apple, and the seventh part of a seventh part divided again until what part remains can be seen nor touched nor tasted.

6. The ignorant eye shall not see the temple from within, 7. for it is vast as all the manifest universe.

8. Beyond life, beyond death is the temple, for it is the temple of the Spirit.

9. About the temple and encompassing it round grows a garden rank with thorns, which are the thorns of khear.

10. Know well your own heart, and the thorns that grow therein; for without that knowledge shall you rarely pass through into the temple, 11. Nor shall you cultivate the flowers of the Spirit which alone make life sweet with their fragrance.

12. For the Spirit is One, and I am the Spirit. 13. And you are the Spirit also, in the innermost temple of your heart.

14. And She who is the Spirit, My Mother, holds out Her hands to you in happiness beyond all knowing and joy beyond expression of all words.

15. And truly, all sweetness is the far-blown scent of this Sweetness; and all Beauty is the pale and dimmed reflection of

this Beauty; and all music but the faint and distant echo of this Music.

16. And when you think upon this Sweetness, will not your heart grow heavy in the thought of the harsh thorns that hold you from it? 17. Will not your faults lay heavy on your soul that divide you from Perfection? 18. And that you have frowned upon the laughter of My Mother, will that not cause you now to weep?

19. Let flow your tears, My children, for they are the beginning of joy.

20. For every tear of true repentance shall dissolve away a thorn, and it shall be as though it had not been.

21. But deep are the roots of the thorns, and beyond your power to destroy them, for they are the roots of Death. 22. Therefore place your trust not in the power of your own hands, and be not raised up with the pride of self-possession, 23. But cast yourself down and give yourselves to Me in quiet humbleness. 24. To be raised up is to be cast down, but to be cast down is to be raised up. 25. For I was cast down into the very depths; and even as the tears of My Mother's sorrow raised Me up from death, so shall the tears of My suffering deliver you.

26. Know then your heart and render it to Me; 27. And I shall lead you to the innermost temple of your heart, whose form is the form of a rose.

The Secret of the World

Authorised Version

MY CHILDREN, whose souls are My sisters, I shall speak to you of the things that I have seen.

2. Let none say that the world is good, nor that the world is ill. 3. For I have stood at the highest point of the world and at the lowest; and from each of these can the world be seen, and from no other.

4. The cosmos is a perfect sphere, more lovely than the sun, and yet it is all riven through with khear. 5. All that is was fashioned by My Mother out of the laughter of Her heart and the cunning of Her hands, and all that is very good, more than any soul can know. 6. But khear is not. Khear is naught. Khear is the black abyss that has turned its face from My Mother and has frowned upon the laughter of Her heart.

7. This abyss of khear lies between the world and My Mother, and every soul and She. For every soul is an image of the world.

8. Let none say that the abyss of khear is not evil, for I have journeyed to the heart of the abyss. I have passed through the seven gates of death; and seven swords have passed into My heart, each cleaving more deeply than the last. I have seen the uttermost depths of khear 9. And My soul has cried out in her distress; cried out into the echoless void. Truly, there is no suffering like to this suffering, nor any pain of body or of mind.

10. And you, My children, each of you that gather round Me, each of you in her robe of purest white, each one has this khear within her, and there is not one without it anywhere.

11. For you have also turned from My Mother; each one of you, though remembrance has not potency through the tread of time, has frowned also on the laughter of Her heart.

12. And your souls, your laughing souls, all robed in purest white, that are more lovely than the sun because they are the image of My Mother, are riven through with khear.

13. And your dearest joy must ring as a silver bell that has a crack; sweetly, but never in perfection.

14. Oh, do not say that you are perfect, for then you can not understand either the world or your own selves. 15. Do not say that you are innocent, for that would be to mock My suffering.

16. For I love each of you, and I have proved My love, and shall prove it evermore.

17. For I have conquered death and khear, and I bring to you My conquest. 18. Open your heart to Me, and I shall bring you all the fruit that I have reaped in sorrow.

19. Seek not to conquer Khear alone nor cleave alone to Good, but open your heart to Me, and let Me live through you, for I shall open the way to your true soul, your laughing soul, all robed in white, more lovely than the sun; and through My death shall she be purified.

20. Turn from the evil of the world and come to Me, and I shall lead you to your heart's true home.

21. Come to Me, My children, in the innocence of your hearts, and look upon the beauty of the world; for every thing reflects the glory of Dea.

22. See the world not through the eyes of the world, but through the eyes of the Eternal.

23. Know also that the world is not so solid as it seems, but in truth it is illusion. 24. Change that within you and the world without will change. But seek to change the world, and all of essence will remain the same.

25. And this is the secret of the world that the world would hide from you: that all things lie within the souls of maids, and only High Dea is without.

26. For in order to gain the world, you must give the world away; and in order to attain your desire, you must pass beyond all desire; and in order to find yourself, you must lose yourself; and in order to have Life Eternal, you must go unto death even as I have gone unto death.

27. And this is the secret of the world that all the world will hide from you.

The Clew of Love

Authorised Version

LOVE is the soul of harmony by which all existence is made possible.

2. For the perfect existence of the Spirit, its very nature is Love. The pure soul is in harmony with Dea and with her self and with all things.

3. And for the existence that has fallen from perfection; truly it is the music of Divine harmony that sustains it in the motion of its wholeness.

4. It is Love that holds the drop of dew pendent upon a blade of grass, neither flowing forth in watery profusion, but swelling within the unseen urn of its brief harmony.

5. It is Love that holds the stars within their courses, and all the worlds of the immeasurable cosmos within the harmony of the celestial music.

6. .Truly, all the cycles of the times and the seasons; all the rhythms of the soul and of the mind and of the flesh: truly all these flow from the love of Our Lady, the Maid, that creation may not decompose, each several member flying away into black eternal chaos.

7. For Light is the essence and Love is the form. And it is by Love that the essence of a tree remains a tree. Else might it as lief become a rushing wind or a forkèd lightning flash.

8. How shall the soul attain to Love?

9. Let her open herself to every creature in compassion and in care.

10. Let her seek to do no harm to any being.

11. Let her love extend even to those who do her hurt.

12. For perfect love is perfect knowledge and perfect knowledge is perfect love.

13. Let her know that no creature gains good for herself by any harmful act; for every stone returns to she that throws it in

the fullness of time. And the shaft that her hand releases shall fly a thousand years until it cleave her heart.

14. But she that does a kindly action shall be thrice blessed.

15. Once in the doing of it; for the hand of Dea shall rest upon her.

16. Once in the raising of her soul upon the path toward her Lady.

17. And once in the deed itself; for every rose plucked and sent forth shall come as a gift to her when her heart is weary, and every cup of wine that she gives to another shall quench the thirst of her own lips in the fullness of time.

18. She who gives succour to those who have need prepares a place of safe repose for her soul. And she who turns no creature away surrounds her soul with beauty.

19. For the soul that grows in Love grows ever more lovely, but the soul that turns from Love is repellent of aspect. 20. Let the soul know before all that the greatest love is the love of Dea, and from this love all other loves flow.

21. Let her open herself to her Lady that She may come as a perfect love for Her. Let her learn of our Lady that eternal Love which is our Lady.

22. And she who loves her Lady in perfection shall have perfect love of all Her creatures, even as She.

23. For this is the Love that is perfect knowledge, and the knowledge that is perfect Love.

Note: Déanic thought is governed by the concept of thamë: the Divine Harmony, or Golden Order, that rules all things and is not less "moral" than it is cosmic: "It is love that holds the stars within their courses". This harmony, while it is ruled by Sai Thamë, is closely related to Sai Sushuri, the Divine Love. Thus Sai Thamë and Sai Sushuri are said to be sisters. This passage depicts thamë in its love-aspect and also makes clear its relation to mati, the Divine Light or knowledge, ruled by Sai Mati. Another underlying doctrine of this passage is that the continued existence of the world is made possible only by the loving sacrifice of the Daughter ("Our Lady, the Maid").

Cry Marya

Authorised Version

CRY MARYA; Mother; and in the mists and vapours of illusion, thou hast seized the Real. 2. For She alone existeth. The world is false, and only She is true.

3. If the Truth be comprehended, then is it believed. If the Truth be not believed, it hath not been comprehended.

4. Like to the sea is the Spirit My Mother, and like to the waves upon the sea are all Her creatures. 5. No thing existeth that existeth not in Her. 6. All things are in Her, yet She is not in any thing.

7. The Awakened seeth not things, but seeth only the spirit My Mother, for no thing is outside Her, and all things are nothing save She.

8. The unawakened is she who seeth but fragments: who seeth the waves, but not the sea; who heareth the voice, but not the word; who seeth the light, but not the sun.

9. These fragments, contradictory, impossible, these are the severed substances of the world. How should the Awakened one see these?

10. Cry: Mother, I know that I am one with Thee and all things are one in Thee.

11. Awake me from the dream of separation.

12. All the complexities of the world are but the turnings of a labyrinth, and at the centre is the fiery rose-heart of our Mother, burning with perfect love.

13. If thou wouldst find union with our Mother, know that thou hast never left Her.

14. If thou wouldst escape the veil of matter, know that there is no matter and no veil.

The Way of Simplicity

Authorised Version

UNLESS your souls be simple as the running deer, My children, and your hearts as little children filled with wonder, how shall you attain liberation?

2. Let your ways be gentle as the milk-white dove, and graceful as the gliding of the swallow.

3. For there are ways and rhythms in the course of life, of day and night, of seasons and the moon, by which all life, all thought, all work are governed 4. and these movements are the breath of the Divine, reflected in the highest spheres and every living thing.

5. All nature is a vast and subtle music to which the innocent soul is close attuned.

6. The profane assay to sever themselves from this music, fixing new laws of gain and self-advantage against the law of universal love.

7. Honour in all things the times and the seasons, keeping fast in times of fast with diligence and care; rejoicing in times of feast with generous outpouring.

8. No tree may blossom out of season, nor any flower greet springtime with austerity, but a maid lacking inward control is broken from the rhythm.

9. For her shall there be nor warmth nor cold, shall there be neither light nor darkness.

10. Thamelic life is danced within the music of Eternity, and the pattern of the dance is Wholeness.

11. But without control shall the dance be destroyed; without discipline is the rhythm shattered in a host of discordant fragments.

12. Harmony is the key of life, and innocence the key of harmony

13. She who is in harmony shall be marked by gentleness, by

meekness of spirit and by the pure light of abundant joy shining forth from the inmost cavern of her being.

14. My children, you shall walk upon the world, yet you are the children of heaven; therefore live by the light of the Spirit and not by the light of the world.

15. For the wisdom of innocence shall the profane call mere folly, and the Law of Love move the lips of the sullen to laughter.

16. But the wisdom of the world is folly in the light of the Eternal.

17. Covet you not the riches of the world, but give forth freely of them.

18. Seek you not more than shall maintain your body, nor give your life to the pursuit of wealth;

19. For the wealth of this world shall evanish as the wealth of dreams, but the wealth of the spirit shall be manifest a thousandfold in the worlds to come.

20. Who shall envy the mighty of this world that are the captains of a sinking vessel? The simple heart is heir to wealth beyond all knowing.

21. Love every soul as you love your own self, and give forth freely of all good things of body and of soul.

22. The perfect maid keeps nothing for her own, giving forth all she has; yet the more she is emptied, the fuller she becomes, for the way of harmony is the way of eternal abundance.

23. But she who pursues only earthly riches prepares for herself the path of poverty; for only the poor in soul can be rich in spirit; and only the chaste know ecstasy.

36. What a maid gains, that has she lost, but what she gives freely, that has she gained in perfection.

37. And all this is mere folly to the world.

38. Therefore walk you in simplicity on the world, and let your heart be as the heart of a little child.

39. And that the world laugh at you, count it an honour; that they scorn you, count it a blessing.

40. It is not possible that a flute should play at once two tunes; nor may any maid pursue at once true wisdom and the false.

41. Therefore be you attuned to the music of Eternity, and dance within the rhythm of the Mysteries and the seasons.

42. Let your soul be simple, that she may be the mirror of pure love.

43. For the truth is such that a child may understand it, yet the sage, if she have not simplicity and love, may struggle for it all her life and at the end have nothing.

44. What is your truth if it cannot be shared with a child?

45. For in the eyes of Eternity, how little is the space between an infant and the wisest of the world.

On Our Mother's Love

TAKE HEART, My children, take joy and courage in our Mother.

2. For She that created you also loves you, even to the end of the age.

3. Take heart, though you have turned from Her.

4. For She has not forsaken you, neither are Her eyes filled with anger.

5. And Her hands that have shattered the gates of Hell shall not harm you; that have broken Hell's foundation shall be lain on you in gentleness.

6. Therefore hide yourself not from Her, and put aside the tangled weeds of thought that strive each with the other.

7. For of all things, love is the simplest.

Part IV

CANONICAL HYMNS

Canticle of the Daughter: the *Exaltia*

Our Lady is exalted among the daughters of Heaven.
Radiant Princess, Star of the Sea,
Robed in celestial light.

She abases the cruel and proud
And hearkens to the plea of the lowly.
The foe who denies Her Godhead she overthrows
But blessed is the humblest of Her servants.
She delivers the captive into Her care
And takes the hand of the fallen.
Firm-fixèd is the destiny
Of the monarch who honours Her name.

May the whole world praise Thee, compassionate Princess;
May Thy glory be told of in all the earth.
Let them exalt Thy dominion
And Thy valiant courage
And glorify Thy holy Name.

Have mercy on Thy servant who gives Thee blessing
And take her hand in need and suffering.
In illness and distress, give her the gift of life.
May she go forever in joy and delight
To magnify Thy holy Name
Before all the peoples of the world.

The basis of this hymn is at least 4,000. years old. In its earliest known form it is addressed to Ishtar/Inanna, Who was both Supreme Deity and Sacrificial Saviouress. It is echoed much later in the Magnificat of the Lady Mary.

Canticle of the Mother

There is no thing fairer on the earth than She,
Nor any thing upon the Heaven fairer.
Before Her splendour doth the noonday sun
Burn as the dying embers of a fire.

Mother of all:
Doth not Thy Spirit breathe in all created things?
Is not all darkness scattered by Thy fire?
And but for Thee, would not all cosmos decompose?
Would not the black abyss of chaos swallow all?
And as Thine universal music reins the furthest spheres,
So does it tune the beating of my heart.

For as the running doe longs for the cooling streams,
So is my soul athirst for Thy dear Grace;
And as long hunger brings the limbs to weakness,
Trembles my soul for confluence with Thee.

Have pity on my soul and end her trembling;
Fill her with the good nourishment of Thy love;
For there is no thing other that will cool her fever,
And no way other she shall find content.

O, let my soul be chastened by her suffering,
O, let her cry to Thee in childlike trustfulness,
Let her be humbled in Thy gentle light.

Of mine own self I can accomplish nothing;
Only so far as Thou art acting through me.
How dull my soul is, like the ashes of a fire:
Yet piercèd through with Thine eternal rays,
Is she not radiant as the noonday sun?

There is no thing fairer on the earth than Thee,
Nor any thing upon the Heaven fairer.

Appendix

PRAYERS

Offering of Food

Many Filianists regard eating as a minor sacrament. Food is offered to Dea and thus becomes prasada—*sacred food eaten first by Her.*

Lady of all nature, we offer You this food
Take it and bless it that we may be nourished.

If it is not one's custom to offer food, or if the food seems unsuitable for offering (some Filianists, for example, do not offer beef) the following simple grace may be used:

Lady of all nature, we thank you for the gifts of Your creation
Grant us Your blessing now and eternally.

Daughter of Light

Daughter of Light that reigns as Queen of Heaven,
    all praise and honour we joyfully give to You.
Give us to know that You are by us
    in every act we make.
Teach us obedience and humility
    and joy of heart
      that comes of self-forgetting.
Help us to be clear mirrors of Your Love
    reflecting all the beauty of the world
    for beauty is the echo of Eternity.
Fix our hearts on the Eternal
    and let us not be turned from You by transient things.
Rescue us from the hands of darkness
    that we may serve You with all our being
    here and in Your bright Eternity.

Prayer on Sleeping

Mother, to Whom all the thousands of the days are as one, and yet Who knowest more of the small events of my past day than I; receive my spirit at the ending of the day and protect her through the night.

The Heart Invocation

Marya, O Marya, enter my heart as Thy love

This simple invocation is used repeatedly, often chanted rhythmically. It serves the function both of a mantra of the fundamental MA name of Dea and an invocation to the Supreme Love enter our hearts as Her own devotion, in accordance with the words:
"Of mine own self I can accomplish nothing; only so far as Thou art acting through me" (Canticle of the Mother).

Against Temptation

I am Thy child, Mother, now and eternally:
let my heart turn from these transient things.

CATHOLIC CANONICAL HOURS

These liturgies for worship throughout the day are based on the ancient practice of marking the passage of the hours with prayer: "she praised Her in the morning and at evening and at all the seven hours of the day." Mythos of the Daughter 2:28. *The Christian Church inherited this practice which has been taken up by modern Collyridians (worshipers of the Lady Mary as sole and supreme Deity). They are called Catholic because they are based on a Western tradition which was inherited by Christian Europe from the original religion of Our Mother God. For example, the formula "whose service is perfect freedom" while currently best known in a Christian context was originally used of Dea in the form of Isis.*

These liturgies are offered here for those who wish to worship Dea in the manner of this Western Catholic tradition. We include the three main Offices of Terce, Hemera and Epi-Hemera as well as the offices for wakening and retiring.

LITURGIES FOR THE FIVE HOURS

Office of Aurora (upon awakening)

GLORY be to the Holy and Eternal One: to the Blessed Mother, to the Divine Daughter, and to Dea beyond Form, Who was before the beginning and will be when all the worlds are ended.

Most Holy Lady, we thank thee for the gift of this new dawn. Guide us that we may use these precious hours with wisdom, faith and gentleness. Grant that every moment may be lived unto Thy glory, that we may in all things serve Thee, Whose service is perfect freedom.

> Hail Mary, Fount of Grace
> Lady of earth and Heaven
> Blessed Art Thou by all maidens
> And blessed is Thy most beloved Daughter.
> Holy Mary, Mother and God
> Shelter us fallen ones now
> And in the hour of our death.

Office of the Third Hour (Terce: 9. a.m.)

GLORY be to the Holy and Eternal One: to the Blessed Mother, to the Divine Daughter, and to Dea beyond Form, Who was before the beginning and will be when all the worlds are ended.

O give thanks unto Our Lady, and call upon Her name; tell the people what things She hath done. The hour cometh, and now is, when all true worshippers shall worship the Queen of Heaven in spirit and in truth; for She seeketh such to worship Her.

Holy, almighty, gracious and loving Lady, to Whom all hearts are open, all desires known, and from Whom no secrets are hid; cleanse the thoughts of our hearts by the inspiration of Thy

Holy Spirit, that we may perfectly love Thee, and worthily magnify Thy holy name. Amen.

> Hail Mary, Fount of Grace
> Lady of earth and Heaven
> Blessed Art Thou by all maidens
> And blessed is Thy most beloved Daughter.
> Holy Mary, Mother and God
> Shelter us fallen ones now
> And in the hour of our death.

Office of Hemera: the Sixth Hour (Sext: Noon)

GIVE praise, ye servants of the Eternal;
praise Her majestic Name
Let the Name of Our Lady be blessed,
from this time forth for evermore.
From the rising of the sun to its going down.
let the Name of Our Lady be praised.
The Eternal One is high above all nations,
and Her glory above the heavens.

Glory be to the Holy and Eternal One: to the Blessed Mother, to the Divine Daughter, and to Dea beyond Form, Who was before the beginning and will be when all the worlds are ended.

Our Lady, Thou willst keep in perfect peace those whose minds are fixed on Thee; for in returning and rest we shall be saved; in quietness and trust shall be our strength.

> Hail Mary, Fount of Grace
> Lady of earth and Heaven
> Blessed Art Thou by all maidens
> And blessed is Thy most beloved Daughter.
> Holy Mary, Mother and God
> Shelter us fallen ones now
> And in the hour of our death.

Celestial Mother, Whose peace exceedeth all our understanding: regard not our sins, but the faith of Thy children, and give to us the peace and unity of Thine heavenly Abode. O Universal Mother, shining like the Sun, O Daughter, gentle Moon of our salvation, let us take shelter forever beneath Thy mantle.

Office of Epi-Hemera: Ninth Hour (None: 3. p.m.)

MOST merciful Lady,
we confess that we have sinned against Thy Light
in thought, word, and deed,
by what we have done
and by what we have left undone.
We have turned from Thee to the things of Thy creation;
we have loved our little selves above the Great Self that is Thee
and that shines in our sisters.
We are truly sorry and we humbly repent.
Rescue us from the ungentle winds of werdë;
have mercy on us and forgive us;
that we may delight in Thy sovereign will,
and walk in the Way of Heaven,
to the glory of Thy holy Name. Amen.

Hail Mary, Fount of Grace
Lady of earth and Heaven
Blessed Art Thou by all maidens
And blessed is Thy most beloved Daughter.
Holy Mary, Mother and God
Shelter us fallen ones now
And in the hour of our death.

For Thou, our most gracious Lady Mary, art indeed the true joy and gladness of those who love Thee. Glory to thee, Celestial Mother; the Angels adore Thee by day and by night. Thou art the Mother of the world, the Daughter who saves all beings, the Absolute Deity beyond all form. The wisest of maidens sing Thy praises and the Sun and the Moon adore Thee.

Office of Compline (before retiring)

THE Eternal Lady grant us a peaceful night and a perfect end. Amen.

O Eternal One, make speed to save us.

Our Lady, make haste to help us.

Glory be to the Holy and Eternal One: to the Blessed Mother, to the Divine Daughter, and to Dea beyond Form, Who was before the beginning and will be when all the worlds are ended.

Into Thy hands I commend my spirit, for Thou hast redeemed me, O Eternal One, the Mistress of truth.

Keep us, O Lady, as the apple of Thine eye.

Hide us under the shadow of Thy wings.

Be our light in the darkness, O Lady, and in Thy great mercy defend us from all perils and dangers of this night; for the love of Thine only Daughter, our Saviour.

Be present, most merciful Lady, and protect us through the hours of this night, so that we who are wearied by the changes and chances of this life may rest in Thine eternal changelessness. Amen.

Guide us waking, O Lady, and guard us sleeping; that awake we may watch with Thy Daughter, and asleep we may rest in peace.

Let us bless the Queen of Heaven.

Thanks be to our Lady.

Hail Mary, Fount of Grace
Lady of earth and Heaven
Blessed Art Thou by all maidens
And blessed is Thy most beloved Daughter.
Holy Mary, Mother and God
Shelter us fallen ones now
And in the hour of our death.

The almighty and merciful One: Blessed Mother, Divine Daughter and Dea beyond Form, bless us and keep us
  Amen.

Glossary of Déanic Terms

Annya, Sai: Janya of fire, a reflection of the Sun.

Athamë: Out of thamë, discordant with the Divine Harmony of being, and therefore impure. The opposite of *thamelic*.

Candrë, Sai: Great Janya ruling the Moon. She governs priest-esshood, emotions and imagination and is, on one level, seen as a reflection of the Daughter.

Great Janya: One of the seven Janyati ruling the seven Planetary Principles.

Janya: an Angelic Power (pl. **janyati**).

Khear: means an abyss, but also a crack or gap. The fundamental khear is spoken of in the second chapter of the Mythos of God the Daughter:

2. For a terrible abyss had opened to lie between the world and She, and Her creatures could not look upon Her brightness.

It was precisely to "bridge" this abyss that the Daughter was born. And since the macrocosm of the Total Cosmos is reflected in the microcosm of maid, this abyss, or khear, is found in every human heart, where it is at once that which separates us from Our Mother God and the fundamental "crack" or flaw in our souls.

The Sutra *The Secret of the World* is the Scriptural *locus* for the concept of khear, and how it can be bridged, or healed, only through the Grace of the Daughter. It is is thus a fundamental statement of the Filianic Economy of Salvation.

Mati, Sai: Great Janya ruling Mercury. The Divine Intelligence and source of all earthly intelligence. She rules the Path of Light, or Intellectual Path to Dea (*jnana marga*).

Mati (or Vathë): Solar Intelligence, both Divine and its human continuation, as opposed to the mere lunar reason (which is what the modern West miscalls intelligence).

Matic: Possessing qualities of Sai Mati: Intellectual.

Nescience: The fundamental ignorance that keeps us from the pure Vision of Dea and thus makes possible the world-illusion.

Raya, Sai: Great Janya ruling the Sun. The Greatest of Janyati and a reflection of the Mother.

Raya: "Lady", in the "Lord" sense.

Ranya: Spiritual mistress.

Rayati: (greeting) Hail to the Sun (in thee).

Rhavë, Sai: Great Janya ruling Saturn. Her qualities are firmness, establishment and severity. She is in some senses seen as a reflection of the Dark Mother.

Rhavic: Possessing qualities ruled by Sai Rhavë.

Sitthamë: Personal thamë: the individual thamë, or *métier* of a particular being. Cf. Skt. *svadharma*.

Strivatë: The Thread-Spirit: She Who unites all the worlds of creation "as pearls upon a string". Cf Skt. *Sutratma*.

Sushuri, Sai: Great Janya ruling Venus. She is the Divine Love and the source of all earthly love, *not* to be confused with the carnality associated with Venus in patriarchal usage. She also rules the Love Path to Dea (*bhakti marga*).

Sushuri (or Sucri): Love, having its source in the Divine.

Sushuric: Possessing qualities of Sai Sushuri.

Thamë, Sai: Great Janya ruling Jupiter. She governs the Universal Harmony or Order: the Music of the Spheres. She also rules the Path of Works, or of (ritual) action (*karma marga*).

Thamë : The principle of Order and Harmony applying equally to the order of the stars and to human society. The basis of Déanic and Aristasian science and social order.

Thamelic (older **thamely**): in accordance with the Golden Order of thamë. The opposite of *athamë*.

Vaya, Sai: The Wind Spirit, or Spirit as Breath.

Vikhë, Sai: Great Janya ruling the planet Mars. Courage and protection are her qualities. Dea is seen under Her Vikhelic Form in Scriptures such as the *Devi Bhagavata*, which take Sri Durga (the Hindu Sai Vikhë) as Supreme Dea.

Vikhelic: Pertaining to the qualities ruled by Sai Vikhë, as in "Vikhelic Arts".

Werdë, Sai: Janya of Fate, comprising three Persons: Maia the Spinner, Werdë the Weaver and Kala the Cutter. The Werdi are, in one sense a reflection of the Holy Trinity on the plane of flux and change.

Werdë: Personal fate. Broadly equivalent to the Buddhist/current Western concept of *karma*.

Let her not be held from Dea by any thing that is; for all the things that are have come from nothing and to nothing shall return. But the Mother of all that Is was ever and shall ever be, though time itself shall only last a space.

Let her not trust the ground her feet are set upon and doubt the Ground upon which that ground stands. Let her rather doubt the sea, the sky, the fingers of her hand and the breath of her mouth; for all these things may be illusion, as in some sense they are.

But let her know her Lady as the Truth beyond truth and the Faith beyond faith and doubt.

[the Lady Isis said]: Behold I am come. Thy weeping and prayers have moved me to succour thee. I am She that is the natural Mother of all creation, the Mistress and Governess of all the Elements, the initial Progenitrix of all things... My Name, My Divinity, is adored throughout all the world in various manners, by various customs and under many names: for the Phrygians call Me Pessinuntica, the Mother of All; the Athenians call Me Cecropian Artemis; the Cyprians, Paphian Aphrodite; the Candians, Dictyanna; the Sicilians, Stygian Proserpine; and the Eleusians call me Mother of the Corn. Some call Me Juno, others Bellona of the Battles, and still others Hecate... Leave off thy weeping and lamentation, put away thy sorrow: behold the healthful day which is ordained by My providence, therefore be ready to attend to My commandment.

c. 155. AD

Made in the USA
Charleston, SC
17 April 2012